That's
Amore !

**The Language of Love
for Lovers of Language**

hodestups forelsket · wewe ndiyo barafu wa moyo wangu · moosh bekhoradet

That's
Amore !

The Language of Love
for Lovers of Language

Erin McKean
Introduction by Christopher J. Moore

WALKER & COMPANY
NEW YORK

Published by Walker Publishing Company, Inc., New York
Distributed to the trade by Holtzbrinck Publishers

Conceived and produced by
Elwin Street Limited
144 Liverpool Road
London N1 1LA
www.elwinstreet.com

Copyeditor: Steve Dodson
Illustrator: Neil Packer
Page design: Alchemedia Design

Library of Congress Cataloging-in-Publication Data available
upon request

ISBN–10: 0-8027-1597-4
ISBN–13: 978-0-8027-1597-5

First U.S. edition 2007
Visit Walker & Company's Web site at www.walkerbooks.com

10 9 8 7 6 5 4 3 2 1

Printed in China

Contents

Pronunciation Guide **7**

Introduction **8**

Love at First Sight **12**

Courtship and Seduction **30**

Pain and Rejection **54**

Declarations and Proposals **72**

Terms of Endearment **90**

Word Finder **106**

Acknowledgments **110**

Pronunciation
Guide

T he words in this book are shown phonetically
     pronounced by an English speaker, with the stress shown
     in capital letters. Where some compound words, as in
German, have two stresses, the first will be stronger. Some specific
vowels and consonants are indicated below.

j- *is the French sound j-, a soft, slurred jay.*
dj- *is the English sound j- in jail.*
tch- *is the sound ch- in chatter.*
ch- or -ch *is the sound -ch in Scottish loch.*
-onh *is the nasal French sound on.*
-anh *is the nasal French sound in.*
o *is a short -o- as in hot.*
-oh- *is a long -o- as in comb.*
-a- *is a short -a- as in fat.*
-ay- *is the long -a- as in fake.*
-ah *is a long -a- as in far.*
-i *is a short -i- as in dip.*
-ey- *is a long -i- as in hide.*
-er *is the sound -e as in the.*
-eh *is the short -e- as in let (used where there is
no following consonant.*
-u- *is a short -u- as in put.*

Where translations are marked with single quotation marks,
this indicates a literal translation. Where translations are marked with
double quotation marks, this indicates approximate equivalents.

Introduction

L et's go back to the very beginning. It would be nice to
think that Adam and Eve were in love with each other,
but I rather suspect it was a marriage of convenience.
For obvious reasons, early couplings had much to do with
reproduction and little else, a view that hasn't changed since in
some religious quarters. However, many cultures quickly went
on to refine the business of loving each other, and by the time we
get to Genesis 29, we find a picture of human relationships that
has depth and complexity and sets a pretty high standard even
now. This is the story of young Jacob, sent away from home, really
for cheating on his brother's rights, but purportedly in search of a
wife. He arrives in the country of his uncle by marriage, where
his cousin Rachel, a shepherdess, comes to greet him, and for
Jacob the search is over. He falls head over heels in love, there and
then, with this beautiful girl. Here, then, we have a young fellow
in love, with absolutely nothing to offer, in a strange land, so his
chances of success are nil. Now his uncle Laban is something of a
rascal, and makes Jacob agree to work for him for seven years in
order to marry Rachel. The years of hard labor pass, and at last,
when the time comes, Laban deceives him by sending in
Rachel's older sister on the wedding night. Tricked but
undaunted, Jacob agrees to work for another seven years to be
with Rachel, and patiently gets on with the task until in the end,
and still up against his uncle's machinations, he does succeed in
going off with her back to his own country. Now that's *amore*.

I like this story because, in a fairytale way, it says something
timeless and universal about love. Unlike most ancient stories of

sexual attraction, it isn't simply about leaping on someone you
fancy and dragging her off to your tent. Even the highest Biblical
kings were prone to that, David most famously with Bathsheba.
No, what happened between Jacob and Rachel was about as
humanly interesting as you can get. In the first place, it was a real
coup de foudre that brought them together. But secondly, and
maybe more importantly, it is a story about lasting love. This
couple had to wait fourteen years just to be together. So we can
be fairly sure that what they saw in each other wasn't merely a
fleeting illusion. On the contrary, when you look at the whole
story in the cold light of day, it's a tale about hard work, patience,
and getting on with it, against a background of caring and
devotion. Though when we add in the complication of the girl's
father, what have we got if it isn't *Meet the Parents* directed by
Cecil B. De Mille?

In one and the same story, we find two of the most remarkable
and perpetually fascinating aspects of love: its life-changing
suddenness, and its power of endurance.

Through the chapters that
follow, we take a look at just
how universal these events
are in human relations
around the world and in
different cultures. We begin
with love at first sight,
and end with lifelong
intimacy. In between, we
look in some detail at what
used to be called "the
battle of the sexes," that
wonderful playground,
thoroughly explored

over the centuries in literature and drama, where all the best efforts of society to contain and control human feelings somehow get thrown up in the air when two people look into each other's eyes. This is where we find both the best and worst of human nature, from sheer wickedness and deception, through naughtiness, frivolity, carelessness, desire, allure, attraction, play, and curiosity, to caring, supporting, bonding, loving, and adoring, all in the best possible sense.

This is where words both become the most important thing in the world, and also cease to matter. It is sometimes said that in a perfect relationship words aren't needed, but for most people, at every stage of courtship, "finding the words" is an age-old issue, right from that very first chat-up line to the words that say everything and mean everything. If this is difficult when relating to someone from your own cultural background, think how much harder, or more intriguing and interesting, it is when living out emotions in a culture that's different from yours. On one level, of course, you can make a kind of progress with one of those '*Chat-Up Your Way Around the Globe*' books in the backpack. But at a certain stage of relating, more is needed. If any serious relationship is already, by definition, fraught with problems, imagine how much more difficult it becomes if you can't actually say what you feel. Think of the consequences if you are brave enough to try and express your deepest emotions in your basic Polish and then find out you have insulted your loved one's grandmother. Then you really will be "sweating like a donkey in a suitcase," to use the Polish phrase.

As we step out of our own cultural background, conventions are just as important as words in this game. A British friend of mine working in Spain once happily and innocently dated a Spanish girl for a matter of weeks, enjoying her company enormously, until she asked him home to meet her parents,

which he did with the best will in the world. It was only when
the father asked when they planned to get married that he smelt a
rat. By visiting them, he had become her official *novio* and thus
engaged. As it happened, this was far from his mind at the time.

I wish science had more light to throw on these questions,
but I am afraid that when scientists open their mouth on the
subject my eyebrows go vertical. Recently, I heard a French
psychologist explaining on television that being in love was
"a pathological state." This is rather like saying that being alive is
a pathological state, because everything we do is bringing about
our eventual demise. If being in love is pathological, then I say
we should all die of it, and the sooner the better. Indeed, the
experience of "dying of love" is so common to human
experience that it has informed poetry and music from time
immemorial. Classical Greek kings and queens tortured and
killed themselves for it. Medieval Chinese poets reeled around
drunk under the moon because of it. Romeo and Juliet in
Shakespeare's Italy, and Goethe's Werther in nineteenth-century
Romantic Germany, all literally died of it. Most of these
tragedies had to do with love in an impossible conflict with
society. Love versus duty, as the French tragedians had it.

Most of us needn't go to such extremes these days, though
circumstance is sure to dictate. For most of us, Jacob set the
tone, a few centuries back. It's all about knowing who you
want to be with, then trying to figure out what to do about it,
then doing it.

Christopher J. Moore

Love at First Sight

ove is perhaps one of the few things in life that cannot be planned. No one gets up one morning and says, "Looks like a good day to fall in love!" How many novels and plays (*Pride and Prejudice*, *Much Ado About Nothing*, *The Taming of the Shrew*, and *North and South* to name but a few) revolve around the oversetting of someone's carefully-drawn-up list of qualities considered essential in a mate? Such lists are tempting fate. The plan never goes right. Lifelong anti-smokers find themselves lighting cigarettes for their new amours; conservatives find themselves listening attentively to liberals; followers of rival sports teams (modern Capulets and Montagues if ever there were any) sit side by side in the bleachers. Only love, or at least, strong infatuation, has the power to overturn such natural antipathies in a blink.

Lovers can never hide their new besotted state. The rising blush; the new stammer in the speech of the formerly silver-tongued; the sudden lack of hand–eye coordination (and consequent dropped pencils, keys, and change); the inability to remember common nouns (including one's own name); the inadvertent slamming of elbows and knees into large and previously easily avoided pieces of furniture: all these are the unmistakable signs and symptoms of love. One only needs to add in a new and alarming tendency towards daydreaming

and/or woolgathering, and the diagnosis is complete. An old proverb, as true as most old proverbs and likely truer, states "love and a cough cannot be hid." How old? The Romans said it as *mor tussisque non celantur*, "love and a cough cannot be concealed." This is especially true of love at first sight; anything so powerful cannot help but affect you visibly (and, unfortunately, risibly). Signs of suffering include: making excuses to mention one's new beloved's name; aimless journeys that just happen to venture near their neighborhood, house, or desk; checking for new correspondence more frequently than it could actually be sent. Advanced stages of love-at-first-sight disease may include the writing of poetry, or, for the more modern, weblogs.

But, imagine, for an instant, that scientists discover that love at first sight is preventable—it is nothing more than another virus one could be inoculated against. A single shot would protect from foolish, lovesick behavior and the loss of dignity, common sense, and the unnecessary purchase of new clothes that inevitably follows a painful new crush, as if infatuation were the chicken pox, or mumps. Would you sign up for the shot? Would anyone?

un coup de foudre (French)
[uhnh koo duh FOO-druh]
While the English might be lovestruck, the French experience of falling in love is likened to an overwhelming force of nature: literally translated as 'a bolt of lightning.' Something statistically improbable and, in the case of love, impossible to provoke— there's no romantic equivalent of standing in an open field during a thunderstorm!

colpo di fulmine (Italian)
[KOL-poh dee FOOL-mee-neh]
Unsurprisingly, for such close neighbors, the Italians share a lot of phrases with the French, including the idea that falling in love happens very quickly and strikes to the heart like 'a bolt of lightning.' It is similar for the Germans, *Wie vom Blitz getroffen sien* [vee fom BLITS guh-TROF-uhn zyne]. The Greeks, on the other hand, experience *keravnovolos erotas* [keh-rahv-noh-VOH-lohss EH-roh-tahss], literally 'lightning-thrower love.'

blixtförälskelse (Swedish)
[BLIKST-feur-el-skuhl-suh]
Instead of "love at first sight," the Swedes fall into "immediate love." No seeing required; mere proximity is enough. *Blixtkär* is Swedish for 'struck by lightning.'

el ha dado el flechazo (Spanish)
[el ah DAH-do el flay-TCHAH-so]
Love at first sight in Spain is classical and traditional: it is to be pierced to the heart by *un flechazo* 'an arrow' (presumably shot by Cupid or Eros). This phrase means "he's smitten."

yi jian zhong qing (Chinese)
[ee djee-en djong tching]
"Love at first sight" is also part of Chinese idiom: this phrase literally translates as 'first look fall in love.'

pehli nazar mein pyaar ho gaya (Hindi)
[peh-lee nah-zahr mayn pyahr hoh ga-yah]
India has built an entire film industry on "love at first sight." This phrase is translated as "at first sight, love happened," and this phrase or variations thereof are not exactly rare in Bollywood songs.

ya vlubilsya bez oglyadki (Russian)
[yah vlyoo-BEEL-suh biz ah-GLYAHT-kee]
This Russian expression for "love at first sight" means "I fell in love without looking back." How many lovers promise themselves that they, too, will have no regrets?

šmrkati se (Serbo-Croat)
[SHMERR-kah-tee seh]
Attraction, it is often asserted, is all about the pheromones. In Serbo–Croat, "to sniff or smell each other" is used metaphorically to mean the exchange of significant glances, or catching someone's eye across a crowded room or in the street.

als een blok voor iemand vallen (Dutch)
[ahlss uhn BLOK vohr ee-mahnt VAHL-uh]
English speakers "fall" for someone (occasionally, they do it like a "ton of bricks"). Dutch speakers do it with a different emphasis: they "fall like a block" for someone.

stati na ludi kamen (Serbo-Croat)
[STAH-tee nah LOO-dee KAH-men]

English speakers use the metaphor of "falling in love"
without any reference to what caused their emotional stumble.
The Croatians make the cause explicit: the phrase *stati na ludi
kamen* literally means 'to
step on a crazy stone.'

me traes de nalgas
(Mexican Spanish)
[may TRAH-ess day
NAHL-gahss]

Literally 'you bring
me on my buttocks,'
this informal phrase shows
the position you land in
when you fall in love, or
when someone knocks
you off your feet.

hodestups forelsket
(Norwegian)
[HOH-de-stoops for-ELL-sket]

The Norwegians say *hodestups forelsket*, or a "head
dive into love," to describe the initial phases of a romance.
It conveys a sense of wholehearted commitment to the
relationship, as opposed to a more cautious "dipping a toe" in.
The main risk of diving in headfirst, of course, is that you will
find the water too shallow!

sich Hals über Kopf verlieben (German)
[zikh HALSS oober KOPF fer-LEE-buhn]
You can say that you are "head over heels" in love in English,
and the reversal of the normal arrangement is evocative of the
dislocation strong emotion can bring. In German, though,
you fall "neck over head" in love, which must be even more
uncomfortable, as well as being disturbing to visualize.

retkahtaa (Finnish)
[REHT-kahkh-tah]
In English, we talk about being drunk with love; the Finnish use
the word *retkahtaa* to mean both falling in love and falling off
the wagon. Literally meaning to 'fall down forcefully and
unintentionally,' it also conveys the suddenness and shock that
falling in love can be to some.

mabuk cinta (Indonesian)
[MAH-buk TCHIN-tah]
The lovelorn in Indonesia are literally 'drunk on love.' We have
the same expression in English—or rather, we had; it's obsolete.
A citation for *lovedrunke* in the *OED* from 1390 reads
"Lovedrunke is the meschief Above alle othre the most chief."

mero-mero (Japanese)
[MAIR-oh-mair-oh]
Japanese has an interesting set of onomatopoeic words that
reflect physical states (*gitaigo*) and, less commonly, psychological
states (*gijougo*). They are written in katakana, the syllabic script.
Mero-mero can be translated as "completely in love" or "letting
oneself be limp," so could be an example of both. These kinds of
terms (as you might imagine) are common in manga, and there
is a manga character named Meroko. Meroko is not a traditional

Cupid, God of Love

Cupid, the god of love, is an odd god indeed. Unlike the other gods and goddesses of classical mythology, who are shown as powerful, beautiful, fearsome, or all three, Cupid is usually depicted as a mischievous child, or blindfolded.

The name Cupid most likely comes from the Latin *cupere*, 'desire,' and as his name implies, he is the personification of desire. From the Greek name for Cupid, Eros, we get the word *erotic*; English words related to Cupid have either lost the connotation of sexual desire (*cupidity* is only used to mean 'greed' now, not lust) or are no longer used at all: Byron used *Cupidon* in *Don Juan* to mean "an Adonis" (why didn't he just use Adonis? Perhaps it didn't scan), and the words *cupidous* and *cupidinous*, both meaning 'full of desire,' are now rare.

In his *Anatomy of Melancholy*, Robert Burton says that Phaedrus contended that Cupid's parentage must be so ancient that "no poet could ever find it out." Hesiod believed him to be the son of Terra and Chaos, older than all the gods. In Plato's *Symposium*, it was said that he was the son of Porus (wealth) and Penia (poverty), conceived on the birthday of Venus, which is why Venus and Cupid are so often linked.

In Greek mythology, Eros has a brother, Anteros, who was more specifically the god of mutual love, tenderness, and passion—and the avenger of unrequited love. As such, he fought with Eros, who delighted in instigating unrequited love.

Burton also explains why Cupid is shown the way he is:

> The reason why love [Cupid] was
> painted young, is because young men are most apt to love;
> soft, fair, and fat, because such folks are soonest taken; naked,
> because all true affection is simple and open; he smiles,
> because merry and given to delights; hath a quiver, to show
> his power, none can escape: is blind, because he sees not
> where he strikes, whom he hits.

Cupid, in fact, carries two sets of arrows: one set, tipped with gold, inspires true love and lasting passion; the other, tipped with lead, causes only wantonness and lust in his victims. This was commonly-known mythology in Shakespearean times, when in *A Midsummer Night's Dream*, Hermia promises on Cupid's bow and arrow to keep her tryst with Lysander:

> I swear to thee by Cupid's strongest bow;
> By his best arrow with the golden head ...
> By that which knitteth souls and prospers love

One legend holds that Cupid sharpens his arrows on a grindstone wet with blood—not an image that sits well with the chocolate-box cherub we visualize today.

Japanese name, and is always written in katakana, suggesting it might have an onomatopoeic connotation. There's another reason to think this: Meroko is always falling hopelessly in love.

tragado como media de cartero (Spanish)
[trah-GAH-do koh-mo MAY-dee-ah day kahr-TEH-roh]
The literal meaning of this phrase is 'swallowed like a postman's sock,' but it is used to mean "hopelessly in love." *Tragado*, 'swallowed,' is also slang for "in love." Why a postman's sock? Think of the poor postman, trudging along on his rounds, trying hopelessly to keep his socks from slipping down into his shoes—with about the same amount of success as someone trying not to fall further in love.

vliuben do ushi (Bulgarian)
[VLYOO-ben doh oo-SHEE]
The grinning foolishness of the newly in love is both proverbial and irritating. The Bulgarians note this with the phrase *vliuben do ushi*, 'in love up to the ears.' The Finns are also struck with this kind of foolishness. One might observe, *He ovat korviaan myöten rakastuneita* [heh OH-vaht KOR-vee-ahn MEE-eu-ten RAH-kahs-too-nay-tah], 'They are up to their ears in love.' And over the water in Sweden, the effects of love travel up a little higher, *upp över öronen förälskad* [up eu-vuhr EU-ro-nen FEUR-el-skahd], literally 'up over the ears in love.'

basbasa (Arabic)
[bahs-BAHS-a]
Literally 'to make sheep's eyes.' Why sheep's eyes are associated with amorous glances is unclear. "As an elderly gentleman from Damascus put it, 'It means to look at someone … illegally. In a way designed to cause trouble, to make people talk.'"

sein Blick ging mir durch Mark und Bein (German)
[zyne BLIK ging meer durkh MARK oont BYNE]
There are dirty looks (and if someone looks daggers at you perhaps that is a look that can kill), but a look that "goes through your marrow and bone" is used in German to describe that very intense feeling you can get only from a certain kind of eye contact.

qiubo (Chinese)
[CHEW-boh]
The eyes as signalers of strong feelings, and especially feelings of love, is a pervasive concept across cultures. In China, the clear bright eyes of a beautiful woman—a target for love-struck glances if ever there were one—is referred to by the word *qiubo*, literally 'autumn waves.' *An song qiubo* is often used in China to refer to conveying love by looking at the one you love with beautiful eyes. *An song* literally means 'secretly send.'

fare il filo a qualcuno (Italian)
[fah-ray il FEE-loh ah kwahl-koo-noh]
Literally, 'to do the string to someone,' this phrase means "to check someone out" or "to have your eye on someone." Quite different from what "stringing someone along" means in English!

udari me sliapata nedelia (Bulgarian)
[oo-DAH-ree meh SLYAH-pa-ta neh-DELL-ya]
This phrase, which literally means 'the blind Sunday hit me,' is used in Bulgarian to express the suddenness of falling in love. We are familiar with love being blind—Cupid is often portrayed blindfolded, famously captured by Botticelli in his work *Primavera*—but why Sunday? Perhaps love is slightly more explicable on weekdays?

mi-a rămas sufletul la tine (Romanian)
[mee-ah ruh-MAHSS SOO-fleh-tool lah TEE-neh]
Lovers seem to use the word "soul" more than anyone else
these days, if popular music is anything to go by. This very
romantic Romanian phrase means "my soul has remained
with you," or "my soul is with you," and describes the feeling
of falling in love.

bashert (Yiddish)
[bah-SHEHRT]
A common refrain among those newly in love is that they have
found their "soul mate," the one and only person they are
destined to complete. The word for the idea of two hearts that
were meant to meet in Yiddish is *bashert*, meaning 'fated.'

mune o kogasu (Japanese)
[moo-neh oh koh-GAH-ss]
This phrase means "looking forward to meeting the one
you love," as when one is looking for a soul mate. As with so
many things, the anticipation can be as pleasurable as the
actual event.

mune kyun (Japanese)
[moo-neh kyoong]
The Japanese *mune kyun* is an onomatopoeic word with a very
specific meaning, and was made famous there by an '80s pop
song called "Kimi ni mune kune." It describes the sound of
hearts contracting when lovers meet.

poisoned on (American English)

If you are *poisoned on* someone, you're in love. This was used by
Mark Twain in *Huckleberry Finn*. He used it to describe the
protagonist Tom Sawyer, in the sense of 'enthusiastic': "Do you
reckon Tom Sawyer was satisfied after all them adventures? . . .
No, he was n't. It only just p'isoned him for more."

es funkt/knistert zwischen zwei Menschen (German)

[ess FOONKT/KNIS-tert tsvish-en tsvey MEN-shen]

It's not uncommon in English to describe an atmosphere or
relationship as "electric." The Germans take the idea one step
further when describing the frisson of a new romance, by using
funken, literally "to radio" (as in to broadcast or transmit), or
knistern, "to crackle." Here the erotic and emotional charge
between two people becomes not just perceptible, but
practically audible.

jemandem schlägt das Herz bis zum Hals (German)

[YAY-mahn-duhm shlaykt dahs HAIRTS biss tsoom HAHLSS]

If you have your "heart in your mouth"
in English, you're afraid or nervous.
If your heart is "beating up to
your throat" in German,
you are experiencing
the excitement of
meeting someone
you are instantly
attracted to.

Love Spells and Charms

L ove spells and charms have been used for thousands of years, and range from the innocuous (lighting a candle or keeping basil around the house) to the disgusting (eating the fingernail of the left middle finger of the one you wish to have love you) to the downright silly (using a magnifying glass on January 6 to focus the love around you—because January 6 is the "birthday" of Sherlock Holmes!).

Love potions, whether intended to bind couples supernaturally or simply act as aphrodisiacs, have been made from dozens of different ingredients, none of them efficacious and some of them almost certainly poisonous. The Romans used ambergris, turtle eggs, crickets, and smelts, and an Egyptian papyrus includes references to an ape's eye and an ibis feather. The mandrake root (which was said to resemble the body of a man, and to not only grow only beneath the gallows, but to shriek when it was pulled from the ground, so that harvesters were warned to close their ears with wax lest they be deafened) featured in a number of love potions of the Greeks, as well as in later eras. Other plants thought to be efficacious included henbane and vervain.

Of course, merely mixing up a potion like ordinary cookery would not suffice; there were various incantations that had to be made, and sometimes there was a specific time of day or time of year for their making. Some charms were outrageously elaborate: the making of one "love-cake" required that the maker remove all her clothing in the presence of a witch, and lie

down. A board was strapped to her, on which was placed a small stove. The cake was then baked in the stove, and sent, still warm, to the target of her affections. Other, more simple charms included presenting a loved one with an apple that had been carried in your armpit. It is difficult to say which would have been more warmly received.

One terrible Irish lovespell required a strip of skin taken from a male corpse, nine days buried. It had to be cut with a black-handled knife, and tied around the upper arm of the intended victim while he (it was almost always a he) was sleeping. When the victim awoke (the skin having been removed) he would be in love with the spell-caster, and remain so unless and until the skin was destroyed or burnt. Children of such marriages are said to have a black mark around their wrist.

In addition to charms and spells to produce love, there were also ones to drive it away. Sweethearts were warned not to give each other anything sharp, such as knives or scissors, in case their love was cut.

netsu wo ageru (Japanese)
[net-SOO-oh ah-gair-oo]
This phrase, literally 'raises his/her temperature,' means that you like someone so much that their mere presence causes you to blush.

prendere una sbandata per qualcuno (Italian)
[PREN-deh-ray oo-nah zbahn-DAH-tah pair kwahl-koo-noh]
This phrase literally means 'to skid out of control for someone' and is used to talk about having a terrible, unstoppable crush.

avoir le béguin pour quelqu'un (French)
[ah-vwahr luh bay-GENH poor kel-kuhnh]
The French word *béguin*, meaning 'infatuation,' escaped from a nunnery. The Beguines were a twelfth-century Catholic lay order founded in the Netherlands, whose members, unlike most "brides of Christ," were allowed to leave the order to marry if they wished. (One feels for the second husbands of the then ex-wives of Christ—not many men could suffer the comparison.) The phrase *avoir le béguin* is the French equivalent of our painful-sounding "crush."

ho preso una cotta (Italian)
[oh PRAY-soh oo-nah KOT-tah]
If, in English, the way to a man's heart is through his stomach, Italians have an expression that says what it's like to be on the receiving end. *Ho preso una cotta* literally means 'I've taken something cooked,' but is used in the same way English speakers use "I have a crush."

get one's nose open (AAVE)

In black English (usually called African American Vernacular English, or AAVE), someone who is infatuated has "got his nose open." It can also mean to be vulnerable, like someone in love.

kalverliefde (Dutch)
[KAHL-vuhr-LEEF-duh]

Literally meaning 'calf-love,' which is a phrase also used in English to mean a romantic attachment between a boy and a girl, or any kind of immature romantic feeling. English also uses the expression "puppy love" for the same thing—the common idea, perhaps, being the wobbliness and unsteadiness of newborn calves, newborn puppies, and young people in their first relationships.

cinta monyet (Indonesian)
[TCHIN-tah MON-yet]

In Indonesia, the bumbling young love that the English call "puppy love" or "calf love" is called "monkey love."

mamihlapinatapai (Yaghan language of Tierra del Fuego, which is now extinct)
[mah-mee-lah-pee-nah-tah-PYE]

Listed in the *Guinness Book of World Records* as the "most succinct word," this expresses the befuddlement that can strike us when love at first sight hits. It describes the sensation of being 'at a loss which way to go.'

fartshadet (Yiddish)
[far-TCHAH-duht]

The Yiddish word *fartshadet*, in addition to meaning 'confused, dizzy, dopey' or 'having a headache,' also means 'smitten,' 'charmed,' or 'beguiled.' *Fartshadet* is related to a Slavic root, *chad*, that means 'smoke' or 'a daze.'

vzema mi uma (Bulgarian)
[VZAY-mah mee oo-MUH]

"I'm mad about you." "You drive me crazy." The idea of love superseding reason is perfectly familiar. The Bulgarians understand that being in love can feel like you've lost your mind, and use the phrase *vzema mi uma*, which means 'took away my brain,' to describe a strong feeling of attraction on first sight.

suki de tamaranai (Japanese)
[ss-KEE-deh tah-mah-rah-NAH-ee]

This Japanese phrase is used to mean liking or loving someone or something so much that you can't stand it. It's close to the English "she drives me crazy."

ich hab mich in dich vernarrt (German)
[ikh hap mikh in dikh fer-NAHRT]

In German, this is an informal way to say "I'm crazy about you; I'm besotted; I'm infatuated." Or, perhaps, "I'm nuts for you"— but perhaps only if the nuts are hazelnuts.

ya poteryal pokoy i rassudok (Russian)

[yah puh-tir-YAHL pah-KOY ee rah-SOO-duhk]

This Russian equivalent of being "madly in love" adds one more element. Literally translated, this means 'I lost [my] peace and reason.' Not only has love made you lose your mind, it took your peace of mind, too.

ya soshel s uma ot lyubvi (Russian)

[yah sah-SHAWL soo-MAH aht lyoob-VEE]

Anna Karenina is possibly literature's most famous example of one driven to extremes by love, and possibly the best exemplar of *ya soshel s uma ot lyubvi*, losing your mind for love. Literally, this phrase means 'I went out of [my] mind from love.'

rwy'n dwli arnat ti (Welsh)

[roo-in DOO-lee AHR-naht tee]

The Welsh phrase *rwy'n dwli arnat ti* literally means 'I'm stupid on you,' adding Welsh to the list of languages that equate falling in love with the loss of rational thought.

jō ga utsuru (Japanese)

[joh gah oo-TSOO-roo]

Literally meaning 'to be infected with feelings,' it implies that falling in love has happened more or less against the speaker's will, perhaps because of proximity.

vernarrt

Courtship
and Seduction

C ourtship, flirting, and seduction seem as if they are all closely related; siblings, at least, or facets of the same glittering gem, and certainly all filed under "Relationships: Human," but on close inspection the differences are startling. Rather than being a progression, courtship, flirting, and seduction seem to be on parallel tracks, with little, if any, switching between them. Think of what's implied by calling someone "courtly," a "terrible flirt," or "seductive," and then try to imagine all three applied to one person—hard to manage!

Courtship, the most presentable of the three, arrives on time at the front door, bearing flowers. Courtship wears a tie. Courtship not only meets your parents, but calls your father "Sir" and compliments your mother's cooking. In fact, courtship doesn't mind (at least, not right now) that you laugh just like your mother. Courtship takes you out for dinner; courtship is at great pains to convince you that his intentions are honorable. Courtship likes Sunday walks and dinners at home with a video: dress rehearsals for a life built together. Courtship talks about getting a puppy.

Flirting can lead to courtship, but flirting should really be an Olympic sport. The best flirts from each country should show up every four years and compete. Of course, the flirting Olympians wouldn't wear the baggy official tracksuit of their fellow countrymen and women—there would be specially designed

outfits, much like those of the ice-skaters (although, one hopes, with fewer sequins, at least for the men). Only as an Olympic event would we see flirting as the recreation that many consider it to be—a lighthearted way of interacting with others that includes, but doesn't demand, the possibility of a deeper attraction.

Seduction, though, is much darker. Seduction doesn't have honorable intentions, or the implied partnership that flirtation does; one flirts with someone, but one is seduced. Seduction is done to you, not with you. If you have to be seduced, you're not entirely a willing partner, for one reason or another. There's an element of malice to seduction, a hint of manipulation, a strong intimation of someone pulling strings and pushing buttons—buttons that the poor victim may or may not even know he had. A flirt is mostly harmless, while a seducer is a bad, bad man or a hard, heartless woman. Your son or daughter can certainly flirt under your watchful eye (although they most likely would shudder at the thought), but seduction requires a space and time apart from all observers, and preferably one that offers soft lighting and at least one of the following: alcohol, a really, really nice stereo, and some article of clothing trimmed in marabou.

amoroso (Italian)
[ah-moh-ROH-soh]
This is now an old-fashioned word for "lover" in Italian, having been mostly supplanted by *un uomo inamorato*; a man in love, rather than a lover. Gone are the days when a man was a lover first and a man second!

Frauendienst (German)
[FROW-uhn-deenst]
From the German *Frau*, 'woman' and *Dienst*, 'service,' this means "exaggerated chivalry." The term comes specifically from the title of the mid-thirteenth-century *Frauendienst*, by Ulrich von Lichtenstein, a description of the extraordinary tasks required of him by his mistress. He had his cleft lip operated on (because she disliked his appearance), and he cut off his own finger and sent it to her to prove that he could suffer for her sake.

billet-doux (French/English)
[bee-yeh DOO/bill-ay DOO]
Literally a 'sweet note' in French, this term is now used mostly jokingly, but in earlier eras *billet-doux* were serious business. In fact, an 1841 manual (*Hints on Letter-Writing*) declares that "As a matter of prudence, all promises should be carefully made, and always with strict regard to truth and reason. In honourable minds courtship is always regarded as the porch to marriage, and the lover should promise nothing the husband would hesitate to perform." In other words, a *billet-doux*, however laden with sweet words, may someday become a contract!

bi yue xiu hua (Chinese)
[bee yu-eh shyoh hwah]
This expression comes from a well-known Chinese poem which
describes (as so many poems do) a woman's beauty. This particular
one suggests that this particular woman outshines the moon and
puts the flowers to shame. *Bi yue* means 'close the moon'; *xiu hua*
means 'shame the flowers.' Another expression from the same
poem, *chen yu luo yan*, goes on to say that the woman's face is so
incredibly beautiful that fish sink out of sight and the flying
crane leaves the sky, hiding themselves to avoid comparisons.
When used now, as allusions, these expressions imply that a
woman has a classic and elegant beauty.

pelar la pava (Spanish)
[peh-LAHR lah PAH-vah]
This verb, literally translated as 'to pluck the turkey,' means
"to flirt by a window." The (highly suspect) story behind this
goes like so: A woman directed her servant girl to pluck a turkey
for a feast. The girl went to the window (perhaps for better
light?) and before long her sweetheart came by, saw her in the
window, a vision of turkey feathers and loveliness, and they
began to flirt. The implication is that someone who is invited to
"pluck the turkey" is allowed to come by and see you anytime.

hacer un gancho (Spanish)
[ah-sair oon GAHN-tchoh]
Literally translated as 'to make a hook,' this means to set
someone up on a blind date. Whether the imagery is of a worm
on a hook, or of an old-time vaudeville hook used to pull
performers off the stage, is up to the individual hearer.

aufreißen (German)
[OWF-rye-suhn]

The German equivalent of "to pick someone up" (as in at a bar), has a disturbing literal translation: 'to tear open, to open up.' It makes the object of pursuit seem like a snack-food package served alongside the beer.

rimorchiare (Italian)
[ree-mor-KYAH-ray]

Literally 'to tow,' *rimorchiare* is a slang term meaning "to pick up"—picking up not broken-down vehicles from the street, but attractive persons from a bar.

comerle la oreja (Spanish)
[koh-MAIR-lay lah o-RAY-khah]

Literally 'eating his/her ear,' this means "chatting someone up." It's the Spanish approach from a masculine point of view and "eating," in slang terms, implies persistence. The somewhat sporty term *poner el anzuelo* [poh-NAIR el ahn-SWAY-loh] literally means 'to lay the bait'; it describes the process of seeing someone you like and letting them know you are interested.

hiza o majieru (Japanese)
[hee-zah oh mah-djee-AIR-oo]

This phrase means "to have a talk." However, Japanese words are heavy with multiple meanings.

This particular conversation's intimacy is conveyed by the literal meaning of this phrase, 'to mingle knees with one another.'

xiyyet (Dardja, Algeria)
[KHEE-yuht]
When men are said to be *xiyyet*, 'sewing,' in Algeria, they are trying to win over a girl, especially by talking to her. Perhaps all their "sewing" is also "making something up out of whole cloth"?

é boa/bom como o milho (Portuguese)
[ay BOH-ah/BONH ko-moo oo MEEL-yoo]
Hearing 'you're as good as corn' in Portugal shouldn't disconcert you—it means "you're very good-looking." Likewise, a woman hearing *miuda grossa* [mee-OO-dah GROW-sah] shouldn't deliver a swift slap to the speaker. Used mainly in northern Portugal, it translates literally as 'thick' (as in girth) and also means "beautiful."

Schnitte (German)
[SHNIT-uh]
Schnitte literally means 'slice of bread,' and it is used by both men and women to refer to a very good-looking person—a gender-neutral term for what in American English might be "a tomato" or "beefcake." The Germans are not the only ones who use this metaphor. In Portuguese, you would say *é um grande pão*—'he is a great big piece of bread'—to describe an attractive man.

faire la bouche en coeur (French)
[fair lah boosh anh KEUR]
This French phrase, which means "to flirt, play coy," is literally translated as 'to make your mouth into a heart.' Similarly, in

Courting Rituals

Courtship is an old-fashioned word, but the practices and rituals that fall under that heading are endlessly fascinating, and much has been written (whether true or not) of the exotic courtship traditions of others.

For instance, in Tenejapa, a Mayan community outside of Chiapas, Mexico, the courtship begins when a boy throws orange peels at the object of his affection; she responds by throwing rocks at him—a pattern familiar to anyone in Western culture who ever attended school.

Among the Hmong people of Southeast Asia, there is a New Year's Day practice where boys and girls throw a ball back and forth to show their interest in each other.

Supposedly, in Ibuzo, Nigeria, if a man managed to cut off a lock of hair from a girl's head, however small, she was automatically engaged to him, and, in fact, was barred from ever marrying another.

An 1830s account of travel in China explains that marriages there

were arranged when the husband- and wife-to-be were still children, and could not be formalized without a contract signed while chewing betel-nut leaves, the betel being an essential part of the whole affair (which seems akin to someone studying modern life declaring that no courtship could begin without the ritual consumption of a cup of coffee!)

The ancient Scythians were supposed to have had a turn-about-is-fair play ritual, whereby the man who desired a woman had to fight her in single combat. If he won, she became his wife and slave; if she was victorious, he was enslaved.

An 1855 source, discussing an unnamed "Indian tribe," describes a custom where the "brave," wishing to take a woman as his wife, entered her "wigwam" with a lit candle. If she blew out the candle, she was considered to have given her consent.

The West European male tends to woo from below: the lover singing or playing a serenade at night from beneath the window of the beloved. The lover's song, known in German as *Ständchen*, in Italian as *serenata*, and in French as *sérénade*, owes its widespread fame to the balcony scene from Shakespeare's *Romeo and Juliet*.

It's tempting to speculate how our modern-day rituals could be interpreted by the archaeologists and anthropologists of the far future. Would Internet dating sites be considered ritual matchmakers, without which young people were forbidden to meet? Would the borrowing of favorite T-shirts be put on the same level as diamond rings, considering that both are customarily returned when an engagement is broken off?

English, a particularly attractive shape to the lips is called a "Cupid's bow."

mei mu chuan qing (Chinese)
[may moo tchuan tching]
Meaning 'brow and eyes communicate love,' this phrase is used where English speakers would talk about "beseeching glances" or "longing looks"—trying to communicate with one's eyes what cannot be said.

ligar (Spanish)
[lee-GAHR]
The modern Spanish verb *ligar*, literally 'to tie,' is closest to the British English "pull" (for Americans, "pick up"; when Brits are "on the pull," they are out in bars chatting up potential romantic partners). *Un ligón de playa* is, to use another English idiom, a "beach shark." A much nicer word for a flirt is *un picaflor*—a "flower picker."

avoir un coeur d'artichaut (French)
[ah-vwahr uhnh keur dahr-tee-SHOH]
A fickle flirt in French is said to have an 'artichoke heart,' perhaps with a leaf for every girl he meets? Someone with a strong appetite for love (not to say eager) could be described as *un chaud lapin*—'one hot rabbit.'

la drague (French)
[lah DRAHG]
Literally 'dredging,' this is the art of picking someone (nearly always a woman) up—the one doing the pulling (always male) is *un dragueur*, a term that is used admiringly by other men, and somewhat accusingly by women.

kamaki (Greek)
[kah-MAH-kee]
Literally 'harpoon,' a *kamaki* is a man who spends his time
"fishing" for young women—a flirt.

pokata (Finnish)
[PO-kah-tah]
This word means both 'to bow' (as in genuflect) and 'to pick up.'
And, although explaining figurative language is anything but an
exact science, the connection here has been posited that, when
asking someone to dance (a common pickup maneuver), you
bow subtly.

bercumbu-cumbuan (Indonesian)
[ber-tchum-boo-tchum-BOO-ahn]
Flirting is ninety percent talk and only ten percent action.
Bercumbu-cumbuan, Indonesian for "flirting," literally means
'sweet talk' or 'loving words.'

een beschuitje met hem willen eten (Dutch)
[uhn buh-SKHUEY-tuh met uhm vill-uh AY-tuh]
This is literally 'I want to eat a rusklet (or Dutch rusk) with
him'—but not just any someone, a specific attractive person.
(A rusklet, or Dutch rusk, is a kind of crispbread that is often
eaten at breakfast.) In the form 'I would like to eat a rusklet with
you,' this is similar to the corny English pickup line "Baby, what
would you like for breakfast?" (or "How do you like your
eggs?") when used the night before. This phrase was a very
successful advertisement for the Dutch company Bolletje; and,
shopping for breakfast foods being a notably female task, this
phrase is used mostly by women to men.

faire la coquette (French)
[fair lah koh-KETT]
This term, applies to a woman (or less commonly, as *faire le coquet*, to a man) who sets out to make sexual or romantic overtures by her appearance or gestures: in other words, a determined flirt. Surprisingly (given our stereotypes about the French), it is not a compliment, and suggests frivolity and a wish to seduce and make conquests rather than any desire to have what killjoys call "a mature romantic relationship." The Spanish express a similar sentiment with *coquetear*.

fusto (Italian)
[FOOS-toh]
If, in a sunny Italian piazza, you come across a showily–dressed man engaged in any form of macho display (feats of physical strength, flaunting of high–powered vehicles, etc.) you can use the word *fusto* as dismissively as you like. Literally, 'stalk.'

honeyfuggler (American English)
A *honeyfuggler* is a flatterer, someone out to deceive you with sweet talk (thus the "honey"). *Honeyfuggling* (sometimes also *honeyfuddling*) is public displays of affection. Occasionally, the kissing will be so long and protracted that someone will have to say "he's kissing her like a cow pulling her foot out of the mud"—slowly, and with lots of squelching.

ir embalado hacia alguien (Spanish)
[eer em-bah-LAH-doh ah-syah AHL-gyen]
Meaning 'to go to someone all wrapped/packaged up,' this is the Spanish equivalent of "making a beeline for someone." It is used to describe someone rushing over to someone they find really attractive.

Schwarm (German)
[shvahrm]

Schwarm is a colloquial term that describes an uncontrollable attraction to someone—to use an English cliché, you are drawn to them like a moth to a flame. *Schwarm* can also refer to the way a shoal of fish swim (or swarm) together, although someone who can be described with *Schwarm* would probably not react kindly to the usual romantic reminder that there are "other fish in the sea."

siúl amach le duine (Irish)
[shool uh-MAHKH li din-i]

This literally translates as 'walking out with a person,' and is used mostly by the older generation to describe dating—it's roughly equivalent to the equally old-fashioned British *stepping out* and the American *going steady*.

tipyn o foi/tipyn o ferch (Welsh)
[TIP-in o VOY/TIP-in o VERKH]

These two phrases, *tipyn o foi* or *tipyn o ferch*, literally mean 'a bit of a boy' and 'a bit of a girl,' and describe people who are particularly flirtatious and charming. Irish English uses a similar type of vernacular. Dating is described as 'doing a line' and the equivalent of the American English 'going steady' is 'doing a strong line.'

The Language of Flowers

The language of flowers, also called floriography, is said to have arisen in the East, where women were kept in seclusion. By encoding their messages in bouquets of flowers, they could communicate when written methods would fail either through interception or illiteracy. In 1718, Lady Mary Wortley Montague, wife of the British ambassador to Constantinople, sent to her friend Lady Rich an example of "a Turkish love-letter," about which she wrote: "There is no color, no flower, no weed, no fruit, herb, pebble, or feather that has not a verse belonging to it; and you may quarrel, reproach, or send letters of passion, friendship, or civility, without ever inking your fingers." The language supposedly spread in France through the offices of Aubrey de la Mortraie, who had accompanied Charles XII of Sweden during his exile in Turkey.

The language of flowers reached the height of popularity in the Victorian era, when learning that asphodel meant "my thoughts follow thee beyond the grave" and chickweed signified "let us meet again" was part of every well-brought-up girl's education, and woe to the suitor who confused the spiderwort ("Esteem, not love") with phlox ("Our souls are one").

Carefully chosen bouquets—"tussie mussies"—were put together and sent to represent unspoken feelings, or just as a fad. Few people today select their bouquets with reference to the language of flowers, but some connotations live on: red roses are still preferred for declarations of love (and, less often, yellow for friendship). A popular arrangement for weddings consists of baby's breath, ferns, and roses. The roses for love, of course, the baby's breath to signal that it is everlasting, and the ferns for sincerity. Here are some of the most commonly used examples:

Acacia: *Secret love*

Ambrosia: *Love returned*

Anemone: *Unfading love*

Arbutus: *Only love*

Baby's breath: *Everlasting love*

Bluebell: *Constancy*

Butterfly weed: *Let me go*

Carnation (pink): *I'll never forget you*

Carnation (red): *My heart aches for you*

Carnation (yellow): *Rejection*

Chrysanthemum (red): *I love*

Chrysanthemum (yellow): *Slighted love*

Clover (four-leaved): *Be mine*

Fern: *Sincerity*

Forget-me-not: *True love*

Gladiolus: *Love at first sight*

Jonquil: *Return of affection*

Lemon balm: *Brings love*

Lemon verbena: *Attracts opposite sex*

Mistletoe: *Kiss me*

Myrtle: *Love, Hebrew emblem of marriage*

Orchid: *Love, beauty*

Rose (red): *Love*

Rose (white): *Eternal love*

Spider flower: *Elope with me*

Sunflower: *Adoration*

Tulip (red): *Declaration of love*

Tulip (yellow): *Hopeless love*

Violet (purple): *You occupy my thoughts*

Viscaria: *Will you dance with me*

du hast mir den Kopf verdreht (German)
[doo hahst meer den KOPF fair-DRAYT]

This phrase literally means 'You have turned my head around.' You can't take your eyes off the object of your affection. (In English, we say that someone attractive "turns heads," but someone who has their head turned has been flattered unduly, and to detrimental effect, not necessarily enchanted.) *Ein Auge auf jemanden werfen* [eyn OW-guh owf YAY-mahn-duhn VAIR-fuhn] literally means to 'to throw an eye on someone.' Your eyes (probably both) follow them, showing how interested you are!

ik zou je op kunnen vreten/je bent om op te vreten (Dutch)
[ik zoh yuh OP KEUN-uh VRAY-tuh/juh bent om OP tuh VRAY-tuh]

Ik zou je op kunnen vreten means 'I could stuff myself with you' or 'you are so stuffable.' In other words, not only does someone want to eat you up; they think you are so delicious that they will overeat.

há mouro na costa (Portuguese)
[ah MOH-roo nah KOSS-tah]

"There's a Moor on the coast!" Obviously a cry of warning—the Moors first invaded Portugal in 711 C.E. and occupied Lisbon and the rest of the country until well into the twelfth century—but no longer of actual Moors. This is exclaimed when someone is in danger of losing their heart.

plámásach (Irish)
[PLAH-mah-sukh]
This Irish word, meaning 'flatter,' has been adopted into Irish English as *plamausing* (spelling is variable), and is used to describe the kind of over-the-top flattery that only a twinkly-eyed Irishman can pull off. You know he doesn't mean it, but you enjoy it anyway! (In business contexts, this can mean "sucking up" or "brown-nosing.")

jemanden mit Haut und Haar aufessen wollen (German)
[YAY-mahn-duhn mit HOWT oont HAHR OWF-ess-uhn vol-uhn]
This slightly disturbing German expression translates literally as 'to want to eat someone with their skin and hair.' It implies that you cannot get enough of someone—you want to consume them completely.

tha se fao (Greek)
[thah say FAH-oh]
Tha se fao translates as 'I will eat you.' The phrase suggests that a loved one is absolutely irresistible and is only used when a couple is very intimate. English-speakers also use "I could just eat you up!" but usually only to adorable small children, puppies, and the like.

abrasarse vivo (Spanish)
[ah-brah-SAHR-say VEE-voh]
This Spanish expression literally means 'burn with passion.' Jean de La Fontaine, the cool, satirical seventeenth-century French writer of fables, mentions a Spanish story he tremendously admired where a young man, in order to get to embrace his woman, burns down the house and carries her out through the flames, making it literally a story of "burning passion," as well as arson.

estar tísico/consumido de amor (Spanish)
[ess-tahr TEE-see-koh/con-soo-MEE-doh day ah-MOR]
Estar tísico or *estar consumido de amor* is similar to the English
"consumed by love" and suggests a burning passion. Perhaps
pure biological determinism, based on the fact that arousal
means increased blood flow, is to blame for the prevalence
of "burning love" metaphors in the world's languages?

patimă (Romanian)
[PAH-tee-muh]
Patimă, in Romanian, can mean both 'passion' and 'vice, bad
habit.' So if you love someone with *patimă* you could be saying
that they are either your passion or your addiction.

naazet-ra beram/naazat-ra beravam (Persian)
[NAH-zet-raw BAIR-am/NAH-zet-raw BAIR-av-am]
This phrase is used to convey that one's beloved is so elegant,
so enchanting, and so ravishing that even extremely coy or
coquettish behaviors are made tolerable.

duo ru qing wang (Chinese)
[dwo roo tching wahng]
Meaning 'sunk deep in the net of love,' this phrase is used to
describe people who are deeply in love—they're caught, and
they can't get out, whether they want to or not.

seykhl (Yiddish)
[SAY-khuhl]
Literally 'common sense,' this trait is considered to be an
essential quality of an attractive Jewish man. Not especially
romantic perhaps, but certainly common-sensical. (However,
someone with *Vayzoso's seykhl* is someone with no common

sense at all. Vayzoso was the youngest son of Haman, who
plotted the massacre of the Jews in the Biblical story of Esther.
Vayzoso watched as all his brothers were hanged, and, instead
of making his escape, waited for his turn.)

yasashii (Japanese)
[yah-sah-SHEE]
This quality, roughly translated as "tender," "caring," or "gentle,"
is one that Japanese romantics of both sexes search for in a
partner—the opposite of both he–man macho posturing and
coquettish vixendom.

rouler un patin (French)
[roo-lay uhnh pah-TENH]
Finally, a great mystery revealed: this phrase is how the French
say "to French-kiss"! Literally translated, *Je lui ai roulé un patin*
means 'I rolled a skate to him.'

un beso del 45 (Spanish)
[oon BAY-soh del kwah-ren-tah ee SEENG-koh]
Literally, 'a kiss of the 45' or a kiss lasting as long as a 45 rpm
record (if you're curious, a 7-inch 45 rpm single could run as
long as five and a half minutes). The Spanish equivalent of the
more informal English "necking" is *morrearse*. This means
'to knock chins,' which might happen several times during
un beso del 45.

je t'ai dans la peau/tu me colles à la peau (French)
[zhuh tay danh lah POH/tew muh kol ah la POH]
Translating as 'I've got you in my skin' and 'You stick to my skin,'
these two common French phrases are used in the early, infatuated
stages of a relationship, and mean "I'm crazy about you."

hacer manitas (Spanish)
[ah-SAIR mah-NEE-tahss]
This Spanish idiom translates as 'to make little hands' and captures that early, heady stage of a relationship when a couple cannot bear to be physically separated and are always holding hands.

pitsounakia (Greek)
[peet-soo-NAH-kyah]
'Little pigeons' is used to refer to a couple that engages in public displays of affection, or, conversely, hides away together. Either way, they're ignoring the rest of the group.

melaut (Indonesian)
[muh-LAH-oot]
This word is used to describe two people who are so wrapped up in each other that they have no time or attention for anyone else. Literally translated, it means 'sailing.'

beth amdanon ni'n mynd lan llofft? (Welsh)
[beth ahm-DAH-non neen MIND lahn HLOFT]
In English, when being euphemistic about sex, people often resort to such stock phrases as "would you like to come upstairs for a coffee?" In Welsh, a language that apparently has no literal word for sex, an invitation for a night of passion is "how about we go upstairs?" No actual stairs required.

on s'est mis à poil (French)
[onh say mee ah PWAHL]
One possible consummation of a successful flirtation—though certainly not the only one—can be ending up in bed together. The French equivalent of the slangy English "we got naked" is 'we wore our hair only.'

ty menya prigubil (Russian)
[tee mi-NYAH pree-GOO-bil]
Literally 'you have taken a sip of me,' this phrase is said by the seduced to the seducer.

scopare (Italian)
[skoh-PAH-ray]
Unsurprisingly, in Italian there are several different ways to get across the idea of sex, and, as in English, the euphemisms have various degrees of offensiveness. To *scopare* means 'to sweep' (the broom is implied in the verb and associated with another tool). *Trombare*, 'to play the trumpet,' is another, and *ciulare*, 'to swipe,' is a third. An especially impolite version is *abbiamo trombato come ricci*: where the English do this "like rabbits/bunnies," the Italian animal is the hedgehog—making one think that the passion must be more intense to overcome that animal's natural defenses.

s'envoyer en l'air (French)
[sanh-vwah-yay anh LAIR]
Meaning "to make love," *s'envoyer en l'air* is literally 'to send yourself up in the air.' There is no etymological link between this expression and the English "mile high club."

entyi-pentyi (Hungarian)
[EN-tyee PEN-tyee]
This Hungarian phrase has no literal translation; it is just used to express a friendly willingness to make love. It is also spelled *entyem-pentyem*.

The Kiss

" A kiss is just a kiss," is how the song goes, but what a kiss does has never been simple. Kisses can signal love, affection, respect, or merely greeting. Gamblers kiss their cards to bring luck; mothers kiss skinned knees to take away pain; pages in the French court kissed anything they had to carry. A kiss can wake Sleeping Beauty, or could be "the kiss of death." To *kiss the gunner's daughter* is to be flogged against a cannon on board ship; to *kiss the hare's foot* is to be late for dinner; to *kiss the mistress* is to hit right in the center of a target.

The Romans kissed the robes and rings of their leaders and the statues of Roman gods to demonstrate their submission and respect. They had three types of kisses: the *osculum*, the kiss of friendship; the *basium*, the kiss of passion; and the *savium*, which was the deep, or as we know it, French kiss. However, Cato expelled a Roman named Manilius from the Senate for having kissed his wife in public (presumably with the *basium* or *savium*), and Plutarch, while contending that Cato had been too harsh, remarked that it was disgusting, in any case, to kiss in the presence of third parties. (Cato himself declared that he never embraced his wife except immediately after a loud thunderclap.)

In the Biblical story of Jacob and Esau, Esau greets his brother Jacob, who had tricked him out of his birthright, with a kiss. In the Torah version of this story, the word *vayishakehu* "and he kissed him" is shown with dots above the Hebrew letters, supposedly to show that there is some question as to the sincerity of Esau's kiss. In fact, "a kiss with dots on" is an

expression used by some Slavic Jews to mean "an insincere kiss."

Supposedly, the custom of kissing the Pope's foot arose in the eighth century, when Pope Leo III found that a woman who had kissed his hand (as was the custom up until that time) also squeezed it. In order to prevent such liberties from being taken again, he cut off his hand, and presented his foot for kisses from then on. (The hand was said to have become a holy relic and preserved for centuries without decay, but has since been lost.)

If your lips itch, the superstition goes, you are about to kiss someone, but kisses don't always involve the mouth. We blow kisses with our hands; give butterfly kisses with brushes of the eyelashes against a cheek; and sniff-kisses or Eskimo kisses involve just noses, and no lips at all.

A 1903 book of folklore claims that a kiss on the lips means love; a kiss on the forehead signifies respect for intellect; a kiss on the cheek signifies admiration for beauty;

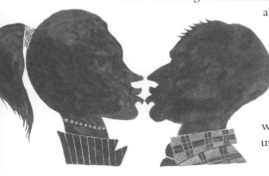

a kiss on the hand shows timidity and homage; and that a kiss on the nose shows awkwardness— which last remains unchanged today.

voetje vrijen (Dutch)
[VOO-tuh VRAY-uh]
This Dutch verb means "rubbing each other's feet together" and literally translates as 'making love with your feet.'

boudoir (French)
[boo-dwahr]
For a term now overlaid with so many carnal connotations, *boudoir* has innocent beginnings. Originally the dressing or sitting room next to a woman's bedroom, *boudoir* derives from the French *bouder*, which literally means 'to pout' or 'to sulk.' A pouting room could be flirtatious; a sulking room seems to be a place where you send a misbehaving child; neither is the scene for seduction that a modern *boudoir* is thought to be.

luí le chéile (Irish)
[LEE li KHAY-li]
Literally 'lying (down) together,' this is a euphemism for "making love."

die Bettgeschichte (German)
[dee BET-guh-shikh-tuh]
Literally 'bed(time) story,' this word is used figuratively to mean a one-night stand.

la petite mort (French)
[lah p'teet MOR]
Originally a medical term, this applied to fainting fits, dizzy spells, and nervous shivers—all of which have also been described as symptoms of love, which is likely why *la petite mort* has transitioned from a clinical term to part of the vocabulary of passion and has come to mean "climax."

hana kalakalai (Hawaiian)
[HAH-nah kah-lah-kah-LAH-ee]
Literally 'carving act,' this noun is used to refer to any casual love affair.

`ashiqa* (Arabic)
[AH-shi-kah]
This verb is used in Arabic to refer to illicit extramarital or premarital sex; one can certainly understand the value of having an unmistakable, highly specific verb in cultures where the consequences of indulging in such behavior can be so drastic.

ci facciamo della storie (Italian)
[tchee faht-TCHAH-moh del-lah STOR-ee-ay]
This phrase, literally translated as 'we have some stories,' means (in Northern Italy, at least) "we're having an affair." You can see it being said over an espresso and with a slight shrug. "What's going on with you and Anna?" "Oh, we have some stories."

red in the comb (American English)
This phrase is used to mean "eager to marry," especially widows or widowers looking for a second marriage. Possibly from the idea that hens' combs get redder when they're laying. This expression is used mainly in the South Midland United States.

Pain and Rejection

~

An early researcher into the psychology of love, the German psychologist Adolf Horwicz (1831–1894) made the observation that "love can only be excited by strong and vivid emotion, and it is almost immaterial whether these emotions are agreeable or disagreeable." He went on to point out, by way of example, that el Cid won the love of his wife, Ximena, by shooting, one by one, all her pet pigeons.

Unlike medieval heroines, we no longer find cruelty to animals romantically appealing, but the idea that love goes hand in hand with pain persists. Limerence, the feeling of uncontrollable infatuation with another person, thrives on a regular alternation of hope and despair; the idea being that one is never sure of where one stands with the object of one's infatuation.

In addition to the pain of uncertainty, the "he loves me, he loves me not" vacillation between joy and despondency, there is the pain that can come of being vulnerable, as one is with one's lover: Cyril Connolly, in *The Unquiet Grave*, says that "There is no pain equal to that which two lovers can inflict on one another." There's also the pain of jealousy (what Milton called "the injured lover's hell"), and the pain of loss; yet, most would agree with what John Dryden wrote:

> Pains of love be sweeter far
> Than all other pleasures are.

Occasionally, the pain of love is physical, not metaphorical:
an English superstition holds that a nosebleed is a sign of love,
especially of love for a person present. There was also the belief that
the flower of the green yarrow could help diagnose another's love;
through a nosebleed, holding the flower, the person would say:

> If my love love me, my nose will bleed now;
> If my love don't love me, it 'ont bleed a drop;
> If my love do love me, 'twill bleed ivery drop.

Of course, the pain of love sometimes spurs people on to
significant non-romantic achievements: Mazeppa, the hero of
both a poem by Byron and a drama of Pushkin's,
started out as just a page in the Polish
court—a page who had the temerity to
begin an affair with the wife of a
Polish count. That count, incensed,
had Mazeppa bound naked to a wild
horse, which was then whipped
out of the town. The horse bolted
all the way to the Ukraine,
where it dropped dead.
Mazeppa, making the best
of things, made friends
with the Cossacks there
(most likely leaving their
wives alone) and in time became the
hetman (ruler) of the Ukraine. From
page to prince, and all for love.

dare il pacco a qualcuno (Italian)
[dah-ray eel PAHK-koh ah kwahl-koo-noh]
To 'give someone the package' is to stand them up (reminiscent of the English "to be left holding the bag"). If you are the unfortunate person being stood up, that phrase is *prendere il pacco micidiale* [PREN–deh–reh eel PAHK–ko mee-tchee-dee-AH–leh]; 'to get the fatal package.' The difference is that being stood up is always seen as more painful to the standee than to the stand–er.

tirare il bidone a qualcuno (Italian)
[tee-RAH-ray eel bee-DOH-nay ah kwahl-koo-noh]
Another way, in Italian, to say that you've stood someone up. (It is beginning to become clear that Italians must spend a great deal of time on street corners consulting their watches.) This one is literally 'to throw the drum can at someone.' What someone who is expecting a date should do with a drum can is unknown.

poser un lapin à quelqu'un (French)
[poh-zay uhnh lah-PENH ah kell-kuhnh]
This French expression for standing someone up on a date translates literally as 'to lay a rabbit on someone.' The poor French rabbit has a history of being associated with underhanded practices; the 1880s phrase *coller un lapin* or *poser un lapin* referred to the practice of not paying a prostitute for her services.

va voir ailleurs si j'y suis (French)
[vah vwahr ah-yeur see zhee swee]
A funny way to tell an unwanted suitor to go away and stop bothering you: borrow the French 'go somewhere else and see if I'm there!' (Which, of course, you won't be.)

no comerse una rosca (Spanish)
[noh koh-MAIR-say oo-nah ROS-kah]
This pitiful expression is, literally, 'to not eat a doughnut,' and
refers to someone who can't seem to get a single phone number
in an entire night on the town.

tirarsela (Italian)
[tee-RAHR-say-lah]
This verb, *tirarselare*, translates literally as 'to pull it oneself,' and is
used of someone who thinks a little too highly of themselves.
As such, it is used to describe unwanted suitors.

llevar a alguien al huerto (Spanish)
[yeh-VAHR ah al-gee-en ahl WAIR-to]
Literally 'leading someone to the orchard,' this phrase is used to
describe the various pretexts made to attract someone of the
opposite sex, ranging in severity from a little extra mascara to
full-on assumed personalities. Whether the orchard is the same
one where Eve offered Adam an apple is unknown.

dostać czarną polewkę (Polish)
[DOH-statch TCHAHR-nonh poh-LEF-kay]
Literally 'to get black soup,' this expression is used by a man to
say that a woman has rejected him. Traditionally, if a man visited
the home of the woman he desired and was served a black soup
(*czernina*) made with goose or duck blood, her parents were
making it clear that they disapproved of him. Any other dish,
and the man could assume that he could press his suit. The
practice lives on only metaphorically. Apparently, black soup
is delicious—though probably not so palatable in this
particular context.

Love Metaphors

A metaphor, as everyone who has struggled through school knows, is a figure of speech where a term or expression usually applied to one thing is applied to another. Much figurative language, many slang terms, and a host of idioms can be seen as metaphorical: *the last leg of a journey*, *he was the boss's mouthpiece*, *she had one foot in the grave*.

Metaphors can also be systematic, where one kind of thing is consistently thought about and spoken of as if it were another kind of thing. For instance, commerce and business are often described in terms used for sports and games: powerful businessmen *play hardball*; instead of talking people *touch base*; and in place of strategies there are *game plans*.

A great deal of the *frisson* we feel upon learning "interesting" phrases in other languages is due to those other languages having different metaphorical structures from our own. For instance, in English we can say "his face was *black* (or *red*, or *white*) with rage"—but we don't say he was *green* with anger, which is perfectly acceptable in French (*Il est vert de colère*). In English, green is saved for *envy*. However, some love metaphors are so pervasive that you find examples of them across many languages.

A quite famous example of this kind of word-mapping of one area over another is the notion that "love is war": He *captured* her heart. She has many *conquests*. You are *overcome* with desire. A much more subtle one is the idea that love is, well, a container. You are *in* love: you are not *on* love, as if it were firm ground underneath your feet; nor are you ever *beside* love

(although love might put you "beside yourself"); you are never *under* love, although love could certainly be metaphorized as a sheltering tree. Only when love is gone do you have a different preposition, and a different metaphorical placement: when love has passed, you are *over* it. Love is so much an *in*, in fact, that you can't walk into love: you must *fall* in it. In Mexican Spanish, you can be said to be not just *in* love, but *colgado/a*—'suspended' or 'hanging' in love, like a ham in a smokehouse.

Love can also be described as a journey. You can be traveling by ship and go *on the rocks*, *run aground*, or *founder*, or it can all be *smooth sailing*; you can talk about your marriage having been a *bumpy road* but you *came through all right*; or you can complain that your relationship *isn't going anywhere* or that you and your partner have to *go your separate ways*.

And although "money can't buy you love," love is also treated as a commodity. You can give someone all your love, or they can steal your heart.

Whether its spoken of in terms of war, commerce, or just as an irresistible force, the feeling of love is the same; it's only the expressions that differ, but they differ in such interesting and evocative ways.

luddevedu (Dutch)
[LEUD-duh-vuh-DEU]
This comes from *liefdesverdriet*, 'pangs of love,' and is used to describe someone else's pain over lost love (not usually one's own). It is less serious than complete heartbreak; little pangs, not a gaping hole.

een blauwtje lopen (Dutch)
[uhn BLAHW-tuh LOH-puh]
In Dutch, 'to walk a small blue' is used to describe being rejected in love; something that might cause an English speaker to sing, rather than walk, the blues.

i kardia mou ekhi gini thripsala (Greek)
[ee kahr-DYAH-moo eh-khee yee-nee THREEP-sah-lah]
'My heart is in fragments' is how Greek speakers say "you broke my heart!" Sometimes it is not just the heart—Greek also uses the phrase *me'ekane khilia komatia*, or 'he/she left me in thousands of pieces.'

mi-ai frânt inima (Romanian)
[mee-eye FRINT EEN-i-mah]
Romanians don't just have their hearts broken (as in the phrase *mi-ai rupt inima* [mee-eye rupt EEN-i-mah]), they can also have their hearts torn or shredded (*frânt* [frint]).

nagligi- (eastern Canadian Inuktitut)
[nah-glee-gee]
Nagligi- is the root for 'love' in eastern Canadian Inuktitut. Linguists believe that this root most likely comes from the proto-language stem *nanglheg-*, which means 'feel pity for' (which is in turn related to the even more basic root *nanget-*

'finish off,' which is also used to mean 'being sick' or 'suffering').
So, even for ancient Eskimos, love hurt.

fordolked of luf-daungere (Middle English)
[for-DOL-ked ov LUV-down-DJAIR]
This phrase is from *Pearl*, an allegorical poem in Middle English
in which the protagonist dreams of his lost love. Following the
tradition of much medieval poetry, the loved one is associated
with Christ and inspires an almost religious devotion. The phrase
literally means 'mortally wounded by love's power.'

estoy hecho/hecha polvo (Spanish, male/female speaker)
[ess-TOY AY-tchoh/AY-tchah POL-voh]
While some crumble, and others fall apart, the Spanish say
'I have become dust' to describe the devastation caused by the
loss of love.

mă sting fără iubirea ei/lui (Romanian)
[muh STINGG fuh-ruh yoo-BEE-ryah yay/looee]
This phrase means 'I extinguish without her/his love,' and
suggests that the other person fuels not only your love, but your
whole existence as well.

patah cinta (Indonesian)
[PAH-tah TCHIN-ta]
When Indonesians are lovelorn, they say they are *patah cinta*,
which literally means 'broken by love.'

patah cinta

òk hàk (Thai)
[ok HAHK]

In Thailand, as in many other places, the heart is considered the metaphorical seat of feelings of love. The Thai phrase *òk hàk* means 'broken-hearted.'

tsebrochen (Yiddish)
[tse-BRO-khuhn]

The Yiddish word *tsebrochen* means not simply 'heartbroken' but 'completely broken,' with the implication that parts are not just broken but missing as well. A *tsebrochener* is a person who is broken and far from whole.

dar calabazas a alguien (Spanish)
[dahr kah-lah-VAH-sahss ah AHL-gyen]

'To give pumpkins to someone' in Spain means to reject their advances, or to end a romantic relationship or an affair.

tener el corazón en la mano (Spanish)
[te-NAIR el ko-rah-SOHN en lah MAH-noh]

In English, we wear our hearts on our sleeves, and the implication is that, while plainly visible, they are fastened on in some way—at least with a safety pin. In Spanish you 'have your heart in your hand,' which makes it seem a lot easier to lose, drop, or break.

se prendre une veste (French)
[suh prahn-dr ewn VEST]
Disappointed suitors in France 'get a jacket'—all they see is the
back of their loved one's jacket walking away. In English, an old
phrase for refusing someone's offer is "give someone the mitten."
Why a mitten? No one really knows. Perhaps it's because a single
mitten is as useless as the word "no" to someone in love.

ta de zi hen piao liang (Chinese)
[tah-duh DZUH huhn PYAO-lyahng]
If you happen to hear the object of your affection say in
Chinese 'her calligraphy is beautiful' don't preen yourself on
it; it's a traditional way to refer to a very ugly woman, and the
equivalent of what is implied by the English phrase "she has a
great personality."

igg (AAVE)
A form of *ignore*, this word is used in the expression *gave him the
igg*—rejected him.

jemandem einen Korb geben (German)
[YAY-mahn-duhm ey-nuhn KORP GAY-buhn]
This expression translates as 'to give a basket to someone,' and
signifies rejection. Its origins are obscure; in fact, *Notes and
Queries* said in 1852 that "Nothing but guesses, and very
unsatisfactory ones, have been given as to the origin of this
expression." The best (if not most provable) story goes that, in
medieval times, a maiden would let down a basket for her
suitor and pull him up to her window. If she liked him, he'd
make the journey easily; if she didn't, she'd let down a flimsy
basket, and at some point on the way up (depending on the
weight of the suitor and the flimsiness of the basket) he'd find

out that his suit was being rejected. Later, the custom changed to the (much safer) one of giving a small bottomless basket to someone whose advances were unappreciated. (Like a reverse Valentine, in a way.) The Poles have a similar phrase with the same meaning: *dostać kosza*.

essere sotto un treno (Italian)
[ESS-sair-ay sot-toh oon TRAY-noh]
Literally 'being under a train,' this phrase is used to describe the pain of breaking up, equating the feeling to being painfully flattened by something you have no control over.

avskjed på grått papir (Norwegian)
[AHV-shed po GROT pah-PEER]
For Norwegians, receiving a letter on gray paper is bad news: it signifies a very formal rejection, such as the loss of a job. The phrase a 'goodbye on gray paper' is used colloquially to mean a way of ending a relationship that leaves no hope of a reconciliation.

beber los vientos por alguien (Spanish)
[beh-VAIR-lohss BYEN-tohss por AHL-gyen]
The expression means "to be crazy about somebody," and it translates as literally 'to drink the winds.' It evokes the idea of the smitten following the one with whom they are besotten, drinking in the air their beloved has moved through.

ag briseadh na gcos i ndiaidh duine (Irish)
[eg BRISH-uh nuh GOS uh-nyah-ee din-i]
Literally 'breaking the legs,' this Irish phrase means "crazy about somebody." Are you breaking your legs chasing after someone, or breaking their legs so that they can't get away?

lyubit' tebya slozhno, ne lyubit'—nevozmozhno
(Russian)
[lyoo-BEET ti-byah SLOZH-nuh, ni lyu-BEET—ni-vuhz-MOZH-nuh]
This expression translates literally as 'it's difficult to love you, and impossible not to love you.'

jō ga fukai (Japanese)
[joh gah foo-KAH-ee]
This phrase means "caring deeply" for someone; it is also used by the object of this deep affection to indicate that someone else's love for you has become a burden and must be shared.

es vercht mir finster in die egen (Yiddish)
[es vehrkht meer FIN-ster in dee AY-guhn]
Love is often described as blind, and in Yiddish the loss of love is also blinding. *Se vercht mir finster in die egen* would be translated in English by the melodramatic "darkness came over my eyes."

razliubit (Russian)
[raz-lyoo-BEET]
This word is simply the Russian for 'to stop loving (or liking).' However, merely by being Russian it evokes a raft of generalizations of Russians as melancholy and emotional, leading *razliubit* to have been mis- or over-translated by the wordy "a feeling someone has for someone he or she once loved but no longer feels the same way about."

sufrir un ataque de cuernos (Latin American Spanish)
[soo-FREER oon ah-TAH-kay day KWAIR-nohs]
This is literally 'to suffer an attack of the horns' and means to feel jealousy. Horns are a traditional symbol of the cuckolded husband.

Love Poetry

I t is highly likely that any word–association test that included the word "love" would get back many replies of "poetry" in response. Love poems are nearly as old as writing itself. Here is an extract from an ancient Egyptian love poem, *The Flower Song*, translated by M. V. Fox.

> To hear your voice is pomegranate wine to me:
> I draw life from hearing it.
> Could I see you with every glance,
> It would be better for me
> Than to eat or to drink.

No discussion of ancient love poetry can fail to mention Sappho. Although only a dozen poems attributed to her survive, this poem, translated by Edwin Marion Cox, is a model of ardor:

> Some say that the fairest thing upon the dark earth is a host of horsemen, and some say a host of foot soldiers, and others again a fleet of ships, but for me it is my beloved.

Catullus is perhaps the best-known of the Roman love poets; his lines *Vivamus, mea Lesbia, atque amemus* ("Let us live, Lesbia, and let us love") were the model for many later poems, including Ben Jonson's "Come my Celia, let us prove / While we can, the sports of love."

John Donne's "The Bait" includes the lines

> Come live with me, and be my love
> And we will some new pleasures prove
> Of golden sands, and crystal brooks,
> With silken lines, and silver hooks.

Robert Burns, one of the best known Scottish poets, wrote his most famous love poem "My luve is like a red, red rose" in 1794:

> O my luve is like a red, red rose,
> That's newly sprung in June:
> O my luve is like the melodie,
> That's sweetly played in tune.
>
> As fair art thou, my bonie lass,
> So deep in luve am I;
> And I will luve thee still, my dear,
> Till a' the seas gang dry.

vanha suola janottaa (Finnish)
[VAHN-hah SOO-oh-lah YAH-not-tah]
This Finnish proverb means 'old salt makes you thirsty.' It is used (especially after running into an ex that one hasn't seen for some time) to imply something a little less serious than what English speakers use "carrying a torch" to mean, suggesting that a taste for something, once acquired, never quite goes away.

cavoli riscaldati (Italian)
[KAH-voh-lee ree-skahl-DAH-tee]
Literally 'reheated cabbage,' this Italian phrase describes a pointless attempt to revive a former love affair, and comes from a proverb: *Cavoli riscaldati né amore ritornato non fu mai buono*— 'neither reheated cabbage nor revived love is ever any good.'

kutimunaykin, llakiymanta mana wañunaypaq (Quechua)
[ku-tee-mu-NIGH-kin lyah-kee-MAHN-tah MAH-nah wah-nyu-NIGH-pakh]
This phrase in Quechua—the most widely spoken native language in South America—means 'please come back, so I do not die from sorrow'; the usual English order is "if you leave me, I will die!"

ya toboy bolna/bolen (Russian, female/male speaker)
[yah tah-BOY bahl-NAH/BAW-lin]
People in love can't sleep. They can't eat. They can't concentrate. The Russians use the phrase *ya toboy bolna/bolen*, which literally means 'I am ill of you,' to describe this well-known phenomenon. *Ti navsegda unes/unesla moy pokoy* [tee nuh-fseg-DAH oo-NYOSS/oo-nis-LAH moy pah-KOY] (male/female addressee) means 'you have stolen my peace,' and is used in the same contexts.

xiang si (Chinese)
[shee-ahng suh]
This is the equivalent of the English "love-sick," literally meaning "thinking about your loved one." In an unhealthily obsessive manner, obviously.

ana l-`alīl w-inta d-dawā (Arabic)
[A-na-l ah-LEEL w-IN-tad DAH-wah]
This phrase means 'I am sick, and you are the cure.' "Love-sickness," as we have it in English, can be both fatal and lifesaving, depending on the inclinations of your intended.

mne tak sladok tvoy plen (Russian)
[mne tahk SLAH-duhk tvoy PLEN]
This poetic declaration literally translates as 'your prison is so sweet,' and is used to express both the joy felt in a loved one's company and the sense that being in love is not entirely voluntary.

ndege wangu karuka mtini (Swahili)
[n-DEH-geh WAHNG-goo kah-ROO-kah m-TEE-nee]
Literally 'my bird flew off the tree.' Flying birds are a common metaphor in Swahili; the taarab song *Sasa Njiwa Kakutoka* ("Now the Dove Has Left You") has the dove not just leaving, but flying to another. (The *taarab* musical tradition mixes Arab, Indian, and Indonesian influences with the classical traditions of Swahili poetry, local rhythm, and melody.)

saudade (Portuguese)
[sow-DAH-dee]

Saudade is a kind of intense nostalgia that only the Portuguese people are supposed to feel or understand. According to Katherine Vaz, who titled her 1994 novel *Saudade*, it is "yearning so intense for those who are missing, or for vanished times or places, that absence is the most profound presence in one's life. A state of being, rather than merely a sentiment." It can also refer to a yearning for a lost lover.

dor (Romanian)
[dor]

Romanian *dor* is very close in meaning to the Portuguese *saudade* and, like *saudade*, represents a feeling more intense than can be described in English, although "yearning" is the word which has the closest sense. The understanding is of an overwhelming and deep longing for somebody which becomes more of a state than an emotion. *Îmi este enorm dor de tine* means "I miss you enormously."

mapenzi ni maua huchanua na kunyauka (Swahili)
[ma-PEN-zee nee ma-OO-ah hoo-tchah-NOO-ah nah koo-nyah-OO-kah]

This poetic, if maudlin, Swahili phrase is literally translated 'love is like a flower, it rises and it dies.' The transience of nature visually represents the often fleeting character of love.

când dragoste nu e (este), nimic nu e (este) (Romanian)
[kind DRAH-goss-tay noo yay (YES-tay), nee-MEEK noo yay (YES-tay)]

One of Romania's most famous novelists, Marin Preda, wrote *când dragoste nu e, nimic nu e*: 'when love isn't there, nothing is there,' an expression that has become proverbial in Romania. (*E* is a shorter form of *este* 'is.') It appears in his last novel, *Cel mai iubit dintre pământeni* ("The Most Beloved of Earthlings"), a scathing critique of Communism.

cargar el arpa (Latin American Spanish)
[kahr-GAHR el AHR-pah]

One of the many pains that can be inflicted by love is that of having to be around couples who are wrapped up in each other (especially when you are still single). This phrase, literally 'to carry the harp,' means to be an unwelcome third party at a lovers' meeting. A similar Spanish phrase is *tocar el violín,* 'to play the violin,' the idea being in both phrases that you are providing background music to the lovers, who are the main event. The Spanish phrase *poner gorro a alguien* is used to describe couples indulging in too public a display of affection; it means 'put the cap on (someone).' Perhaps to cover his eyes?

cargar el arpa

Declarations
and Proposals

~

There is a telling Latin proverb, attributed to either Publilius Syrus or Laberius, which runs *amare et sapere vix deo conceditur*, 'even a god finds it hard to love and be wise at the same time.' In making declarations of love, feeling trumps wisdom every time. The first "I love you" is fraught with tension, whether it's blurted out, inadvertently, on a street corner, or couched in flowery phrases and accompanied by flowers themselves. Succeeding declarations (if the first is returned, or at least not scorned) may become easier and easier, until a very specific declaration may be made: the declaration "I do" at the altar.

One of the problems of making declarations of love is that they are very difficult to bring off successfully. Literature is littered with slightly-off declarations of love, both verbal and non-. In James Thomson's nearly forgotten poem *The Seasons*, Celadon embraces his frightened lover Amelia during a thunderstorm. He reassures her, saying "'Tis safety to be near thee, sure, and thus to clasp perfection," thus jinxing himself, as lightning then struck and killed her. Walter Scott, writing on a book called *The Heroic Romance of the Seventeenth Century*, said that "nothing can be so uninteresting as the frigid extravagance with which these lovers express their passions; or, in their own phrase, nothing can be more freezing than their flames, more

creeping than their flights of passion." In E. M. Forster's *Howards End*, Henry Wilcox makes his stammering proposal of marriage to Margaret Schlegel, and ends it with "I wish I had written instead. Ought I to have written?" Even Jane Austen didn't trust herself to invent romantic declarations: of Mr. Darcy, she merely wrote "he expressed himself on the occasion as sensibly and as warmly as a man violently in love can be supposed to do." Dickens had a lovesick lawyer, Mr. Bradley, turn to a friend for help in writing these appalling verses to use in pressing his suit:

> Whereas on your behalf, one Richard Roe,
> Otherwise Love, with force and arms, to wit,
> Sticks, staves, clubs, bows and arrows, me, John Doe,
> Did shoot and wound, beat, strike, assault, and hit.
> Take notice I propose to institute
> Proceedings legal remedy to find,
> Concerning you, as party to the suit,
> Of me, your loving friend, the undersigned—
> John Doe.

Even the great poets can fail at declarations of love in their private letters; Keats wrote (to Fanny Brawne) "I could die for you. My Creed is Love and you are its only tenet ... My love is selfish. I cannot breathe without you," which sentiments Matthew Arnold called "the love-letter of a surgeon's apprentice ... underbred and ignoble." If Keats couldn't manage it, perhaps we should not feel so bad over our own stumbling efforts?

a minha cara metade (Portuguese)
[ah mee-nyah KAH-rah mi-TAH-dee]
Literally 'the other half of my face,' this is used in the same way that English speakers use the phrases "my better half" or "my other half." Portuguese makes this metaphor even more specific—not just half, but half of the part of you most closely tied to your identity.

a outra metade da laranja (Portuguese)
[ah OH-trah mi-TAH-dee dah lah-RANH-zhah]
The phrase *a outra metade da laranja* (like the one above) is another way to say "my better half" in Portuguese. Its literal translation is 'the other half of the orange,' implying that only with your partner do you make a whole. (Portugal has long been associated with the growth and export of oranges. Persian *nārang* and Arabic *nāranj* show the history of the word, which originated in India with Sanskrit *nāranga* and was brought to Western Europe by the Arabs when they conquered Spain; Greek *portokali* and Turkish *portakal* show the association with Portugal.)

spasibo chto ty est' na svete! (Russian)
[spah-SEE-buh shtuh tee yest nuh SVET-i]
It would rarely, if ever, cross the mind of an English speaker to thank someone for existing, but in Russian, this phrase is common.

te adoro (Spanish)
[tay ah-DOR-oh]

Te adoro—'I adore you.' Who wouldn't want to hear that? The basic expression of love in Spanish is *te quiero* [tay KYEH-roh] (which can be used for any kind of love, but usually platonic, such as that of a mother for a child). Then follows (if all goes well) the poetic *te amo*, which is more emphatic. (*Hacer el amor* is 'to make love.') *Te adoro*, 'I adore you, I worship you,' is the language of the truly besotted lover. And finally, the heights, or depths, of desire, depending on how and when you say it, are expressed with *te deseo*, which means quite simply and basically 'I want you'—in a physical sense.

qorbaanat beravam, fedaayat beshavam (Persian)
[kor-BAWN-et BEH-ra-vam, feh-DAW-yat BEH-sha-vam])
qorbaanet besham/beram [kor-BAWN-et BESH-am/BAIR-am]

This expression means 'may I be sacrificed to thee, may I be thy ransom.' It has two shorter forms: *qorbaanet fedaat* [kor-BAWN-et feh-DAWT], as well as being a whisper of devotion from a mother to a child, is also used to mean "I adore you" between lovers. *Qorbaanet besham* or *qorbaanet beram* literally means 'may I be sacrificed for you,' but has the same connotations that "I would die for you" has in English. (If you happen to get a letter that opens *fedaayat beshavam*, don't worry that you're being stalked: it's also a traditional and entirely emotion-free header in letters addressed to dignitaries, equivalent to "Dear Sir.")

j'ai besoin de tes baisers (French)
[zhay buh-zwenh duh tay beh-ZAY]

Literally 'I need your kisses,' it implies that they are indispensable —not just for love, but for life itself. The French also use the more reserved declaration *mon coeur est a toi*, 'my heart is yours.'

Letters of Love

Nothing is more precious than a love letter, and nothing is more difficult to write, or, rather, more difficult to write *well*. Anyone can put down a string of endearments and call for the immediate consummation of the writer's and reader's desire, but a true example of the art elevates the form from a simple catalog of emotions to near-poetry.

The effective love letter has definite tropes, or themes, that must be engaged. A letter from Pliny the Younger (61–113 C.E.) to his wife is a good example of one of the main ones: the merits of the last letter received:

> You say that you are feeling my absence very much, and your only comfort when I am not there is to hold my writings in your hand and often put them in my place by your side. I like to think that you miss me and find relief in this sort of consolation. I, too, am always reading your letters, and returning to them again and again as if they were new to me—but this only fans the fire of my longing for you. If your letters are so dear to me, you can imagine how I delight in your company; do write as often as you can, although you give me pleasure mingled with pain.

The letters of F. Scott and Zelda Fitzgerald were thankfully preserved, so we can read that Zelda wrote on another theme, that of being unable to live without one's beloved:

How can you think deliberately of life without me—If you should die—O Darling—darling Scot—It'd be like going blind. I know I would, too,—I'd have no purpose in life—just a pretty—decoration. Don't you think I was made for you? I feel like you had me ordered—and I was delivered to you—to be worn. I want you to wear me, like a watch-charm or a buttonhole bouquet—to the world.

A letter from Napoleon to Josephine embodies another main theme, desire for the beloved's person:

A thousand kisses on your eyes, your lips, your tongue, your heart. Most charming of thy sex, what is thy power over me? I am very sick of thy sickness; I have still a burning fever!

Other love-letter themes include jealousy, the loved one's surpassing beauty, and occasionally, renunciation. Examples of those are left as an exercise for the reader.

rwy'n dy garu di (Welsh)
[ROO-een duh GAH-ree dee]
This phrase, which means "I love you," translates word-for-word as 'I'm your love you,' which is oddly satisfying in its literalness. In North Wales the phrase is *Dw i'n dy garu di*. To say "I love you with all my heart" in Welsh, try *mi caraf chwi a'm holl ga/on*.

tha gràdh agam ort (Scots Gaelic)
[hah GRAHGH aguhm ort]
This is literally 'I have love on you,' which sounds almost as if you have accidentally spilled your love over someone and are now apologizing for getting love on their new shirt. An even more intimate way to say "I love you" is *tha gaol mo chridhe agam ort-sa*, which is literally 'I love you with all my heart.'

tá mo chroí istigh inti (Irish)
[taw muh KHREE ish-TEE in-tee]
This phrase (which means "I love her") is literally 'my heart is in her.' Was e. e. cummings thinking of this phrase when he wrote "i carry your heart with me/i carry it in my heart"?

onguboy (Boro)
[on-gu-boy]
Boro, now usually called Bodo, is a Tibeto-Burman language spoken in northeastern India as well in as parts of Nepal, Bhutan, and Bangladesh. *Onguboy* is a very positive term in Bodo, and means "to love from the heart." *Onsra* suggests love with a hint of sadness and translates as "to love for the last time" (literally, 'to arouse the female oracle for the last time'), and *onsay* is the way to say that someone is pretending to be in love.

shindemo ii wa (Japanese)

[sheen-deh-mo EE-wah]

This phrase is literally 'I could die for you,' and the story goes that Futabatei Shimei (1864–1909) used this phrase to mean "I love you" when spoken by a woman in a novel he translated from the Russian. He had to translate it this way, because in his time women in Japan did not say "I love you" directly.

obicham te do bolka (Bulgarian)

[oh-BEE-tchuhm teh doh BOL-kah]

Meaning 'I love you until it hurts,' this is perhaps the strongest declaration of love in Bulgarian. Bulgarian has two words for love: *ljubov* and *obich*, the former expressing passionate feeling and the latter describing a more affectionate relationship. Only *obich* is used for romantic love.

mitn gantsn hartsn (Yiddish)

[mit-uhn GAHNTS-uhn HAHRTS-uhn]

Meaning 'with all my heart,' this is more serious than the same phrase in English. This is not a casual, tossed-off phrase, but a serious statement made, well, wholeheartedly.

yi wang qing shen (Chinese)

[yee wahng tching shuhn]

This is literally 'forever love deep,' but is also used punningly to describe falling in love with someone online, as *yi wang* can also mean 'Internet.'

jeong (Korean)
[juhng]
In Korean *jeong* means a state beyond love; it has been described as "loyalty and commitment without validation, logic, or reason." *Jeong* is a special feeling that is eternal, undying, unchanging—unlike love—and it is felt not to be within each person but existing in a space between them, and serving as an unbreakable connection. A couple can often only be certain to have reached this state by having survived a huge argument. (In Korean, as well, people say "our wife" or "our husband"—implying that the role does not belong so much to the person as to the relationship.)

gua sayang lu (Indonesian)
[goo-ah sah-yahng loo]
Should you lose your heart in Indonesia, this phrase should come in handy: it means "I love you." *Aku cinta padamu* is the form commonly found in pop songs; *cinta* is used strictly for romantic love, while *sayang* can also mean the kind of love a parent has for a child.

alamnaka (Ulwa)
[ah-LAHM-nah-kah]
English speakers who find their niche usually have found a good fit in a job or career. The speakers of Ulwa, an indigenous language of the east coast of Nicaragua, describe the enviable

state of having found their life partner with the term *alamnaka*, which means 'finding one's niche.' The idea seems closer to the ecological sense of *niche*, 'a role or position taken by an organism in its community.'

wewe ndiyo barafu wa moyo wangu (Swahili)
[WEH-weh n-DEE-yo bah-RAH-foo wah MO-yo WAHNG-goo]
Whereas in English the coldhearted are cruel and unfeeling, in Swahili the coldhearted are deeply in love. *Wewe ndiyo barafu wa moyo wangu*, which translates as 'you are ice for my heart,' is a way of expressing a very deep love for someone.

grá mo chroí thú (Irish)
[GRAW muh KHREE hoo]
Ireland has always been the greatest love of the Irish, but occasionally there is some love left over for someone or something else. *Grá mo chroí thú*, 'you are the love of my heart,' expresses great love.

na tebe soshelsa klinom belyi svet (Russian)
[nah ti-BEH sah-SHOL-suh KLEE-nuhm BELL-ee SVEHT]
This phrase is literally translated as 'the wide world came together in a wedge on you,' meaning "you're everything in the world to me." It is the opposite of the common expression *svet ne klinom soshelsya na [tebe]* "[you] aren't the only thing in the world/fish in the sea" (literally 'the world didn't come together in a wedge on you'). *Belyi svet* is emphatic—"the whole wide world" (literally 'white world'), not just the world.

Love festivals

Whether motivated by true love, or by various commercial interests in roses, chocolates, and stuffed animals, most modern cultures have a holiday designed to celebrate love and lovers.

The one most familiar to English speakers is St. Valentine's Day, February 14. The custom of Valentine's Day in England and France probably started in the fourteenth century, and was supposedly the date that birds began mating. The earliest Valentine's poem is Chaucer's *Parliament of Fowls* (1381), in which rival lovebirds quarrel on Valentine's Day.

In Romania, Dragobete, February 24, is the lover's holiday; boys and girls give each other snowdrops. In Slovenia, St. Gregory's Day, March 12, is traditionally said to be "the day when birds get married." That is also the day when children make *gregorč*, little boats carrying candles, to float down streams. These symbolize that the days are getting longer and they no longer need light to work in the evenings.

In China, on the last day of Chinese New Year, girls traditionally write their name and address on a mandarin orange and throw it into the river. They hope that the man of their dreams will find it and seek them out.

In Japan, Valentine's Day is "celebrated" mostly by women, who traditionally give chocolate (called *giri-choko*, or 'obligation chocolate') to men they work with, but not to their spouses or sweethearts. The men are supposed to reciprocate on White Day, March 14, by giving chocolate (especially white chocolate) or

other small gifts to those women who had given them chocolate a month before. Valentine's Day and White Day are also celebrated in South Korea, but are much more an occasion for gift-gifting between sweethearts, and not so much between colleagues and acquaintances.

There's no evidence, other than the nearness of the dates and an air of general debauchery, to associate Valentine's Day with the Roman feast of Lupercalia, which was celebrated on February 15. The Lupercalia was connected with fertility; it had an involved ceremony, which began with the sacrifice of goats. Two noble boys were marked with the goats' blood (and were required to laugh as part of the ritual, something that may have been difficult to pull off). After that, the hides of the goats were cut into strips, and the boys ran around using them as whips on the observers and passersby. Young women, in particular, maneuvered to be hit, as it was believed that the blow not only made them more fertile, but would also make childbirth easier. The Lupercalia continued until 495 C.E., when it was abolished by Pope Gelasius.

dowret begardam (Persian)
[DOW-ret BEH-gar-dam]

This Persian term, which expresses a desire to suffer on someone else's behalf, translates literally as 'may I walk round you.' It stems from an old Iranian folk custom, in which a loved one or lover of a sick person would walk round the patient's bed, repeating "may all your pains, illnesses, and troubles come to me and nothing bad happen to you."

hamnafasam baash (Persian)
[ham-na-FASS-am bawsh]

This very romantic and intimate Persian phrase translates literally as 'be my fellow-breather' and expresses a desire to share everything with someone, right down to the air you breathe.

hubbak yidhawwibni (Arabic)
[HUB-bak yi-dow-WIB-nee]

This phrase means 'your love makes me melt away.'

khatereto mikham (Persian)
[khah-TAIR-eh-toh MEE-kham]

"I care about you deeply" or "I want you." This is normally used by someone who wants a serious, permanent relationship—ideally marriage.

wewe ni wangu tu (Swahili)
[WEH-weh nee WAHNG-goo too]

English speakers often say "I want to make you mine," and "BE MINE" is a common motto on Valentine's Day candy hearts. In Swahili, however, the phrase *wewe ni wangu tu* is fiercely possessive: 'whatever you are you are mine.'

ti voglio bene (Italian)
[tee vo-lyo BEH-neh]
This phrase is a more colloquial way to express your love, a bit short of the grand passion of *ti amo*. *Ti voglio tanto bene* is 'I love you so much,' and slightly stronger. If you want to be way over the top, try *ti amo più che mai*, 'I love you more than ever.'

ich liebe dich (German)
[ikh LEE-buh dikh]
The dictionary will tell you that the most basic declaration of love in German is *Ich liebe dich*, 'I love you.' However, more idiomatic ways to declare yourself *auf Deutsch* are *Ich mag dich*, 'I like you,' and *Ich hab' dich gern*, 'I'm fond of you,' which are both slightly more serious than their English translations would imply. If you want to be more serious still (or sound like a pop song), try *ich brauche dich wie die Luft zum Atmen* [ikh BROW-khuh dikh vee dee LOOFT tsoom AHT-muhn] 'I need you like the air that I breathe.'

di libe kumt noch der khasene (Yiddish)
[dee LEE-buh KUMT nokh der KHAH-suh-nuh]
Literally meaning 'love comes after the wedding,' or "you don't need to fall in love to get married." The suggestion here is that love is a consequence of marriage, not a necessary prelude to it. The first mitzvah (or precept) of the Torah is the command to engage in procreation (Genesis 1:28; 9:1), and the aim of marriage is procreation (as well as companionship). Love, while admirable, is scarcely required.

traer azorrillado/a (Mexican Spanish)
[trah-AIR ah-sor-ree-YAH-doh/dah]
This means "to have someone hopelessly in love with you."
Azorrillado can mean "awed." Another similar phrase is *traer de un ala*, 'to bring by a wing.'

empiernado/a (Venezuelan Spanish)
[em-pee-air-NAH-doh/dah]
This means to be under someone's (sexual) spell. The word
enguayabado/a translates as 'madly in love.'

mizgatisya (Ukrainian)
[miz-GAH-tee-syah]
This is a colloquial word that means 'to make love; to woo.'
It can also mean 'to speak sweet nothings.'

omae hyaku made washa kujuku made, tomo ni shiraga no haeru made (Japanese)
[o-mah-eh hyah-koo mah-deh, wah-shah ku-JOO-ku mah-deh,
TOH-mo-nee shee-rah-GAH-no hah-eh-roo mah-deh]
This phrase is used in wedding ceremonies in Japan, and
means 'Until you're one hundred years old and I'm ninety–nine,
we'll be together until our hair turns white.' The Japanese also
have the proverb *fufu wa nise no chigiri*, 'Marriage is a vow for
two worlds.'

chen pian chih yan mo t'ing (Chinese)
[djen byen djer yen mo ting]
This proverb translates as "take no notice of what you hear said
on the pillow": don't take seriously any declarations or
protestations made in the heat of love.

misschien moeten we dan toch maar trouwen (Dutch)
[mis-KHEEN MOO-tuh vay dahn tokh maar TROW-uh]
This is, roughly, "what the heck—let's get married," and is used
mostly when some external pressure (a more favorable tax
bracket, convenience's sake when a child is on the way, and so
on) is driving the decision, more than any great romantic
longing. More than likely, it's a Dutch woman making the
suggestion, as well.

níl aon leigheas ar an ngrá ach pósadh (Irish)
[neel ayn LAY-uhs er uhng-RAW uhkh POH-suh]
This somewhat cynical proverb states that "The only cure
for love is marriage." In a similar vein is the old Spanish
proverb *Guerra, y caça, y amores, por un plazer mil dolores*, which
means "war, hunting, and love bring a thousand pains for
one pleasure."

masihlalisane (Zulu)
[mah-see-hlah-lee-SAH-neh]
Literally translated as "stay together," this is the word used by
women to refer to their serious boyfriends or partners, especially
ones who contribute financially to their support. (It also seems
to be the name of a traditional food plant much like spinach.)
A woman supported in this way is called an *ishweshwe*
(sometimes translated as "mistress" in English).

qing ren yan li chu xishi (Chinese)
[tching ren yen lee tchoo shee-sher]
Literally, this translates as 'lover's eye produces Xishi,' and means
a man in love with a woman will always think her the most
beautiful woman in the world. Xishi was one of the four great
beauties of China, and is the subject of at least one other
proverb: *dongshi xiao pin*, "aping the beauty's frown." Xishi was
often ill, and would have to walk hunched over and with a
grimace of pain. A local girl, Dongshi, who envied Xishi's
beauty, decided that the best way to emulate Xishi was by aping
how she walked, not realizing that it only made her uglier.

sine ce elong (the Drehu language on Lifou in the Loyalty Islands (part of New Caledonia))
[see-nay shay eh-long]
This term from Drehu (a language of the Loyalty Islands of
New Caledonia) means "my friend" but is literally translated
'piece that plays with me.' Your family is *sineng* or *sinei eni*
(literally 'my piece'). It makes sense: your friends are with you
for fun, but your family—they're with you forever.

myliu (Lithuanian)
[MEE-l(y)oo]
"Like" and "Love" are almost interchangeable in English.
You can love your boyfriend, you can love a movie, you can
love turnips—all with the same word. In Lithuanian, though,
you would use *myliu* only to say "I love you" to your lover
(pronouns are understood when used with verbs). You might
also say *zaviuosi*, 'I admire you' or *alpstu* I'm dying for you,'
but again, only to people, not about things.

I love you (English)

"I love you" is perhaps one of the first phrases one learns when studying a foreign language, whether or not you will ever have any opportunity to say it in an appropriate, non-classroom context. Even Latin, which it is safe to say that very few have used for flirtation in the last several hundred years, starts off new students with *amo, amas, amat:* "I love, you love, he loves." Here are some "I love you"s, both common and unusual, to add to your collection.

> Aztec (Classical): *ni-mitz-tlazo?tla* [nee-mits-tlah-SOH-tlah]
> Afrikaans: *ek het jou life* [ek het yoh LEE-fuh]
> Basque: *maite zaitut* [my-teh sy-toot]
> Esperanto: *mi amas vin* [mee AH-mahs veen]
> Finnish: *minä rakastan sinua* [mee-na RAH-kahs-tahn
> see-noo-ah]
> Hawaiian: *aloha au ia`oe* [ah-LOH-hah ah-oo
> ee-ah-OH-eh]
> Hungarian: *szeretlek* [SAIR-et-lek]
> Japanese: *ai shiteru* [AYE sh'teh-roo]
> Latvian: *es tevi milu!* [es teh-vee MEE-loo]
> Maltese: *inhobbok* [in-HOB-bok]
> Mongolian: *bi chamd khairtai* [bee tchahmd KHAYR-tye]
> Norwegian: *jeg elsker Dig* [yay EL-sker day]
> Polish: *kocham cię* [KOH-khahm tcheh]
> Scots Gaelic: *tha gràdh agam ort* [hah GRAHGH
> ah-guhm ort]
> Swahili: *nakupenda* [nah-koo-PEN-dah]
> Swedish: *jag älskar dig* [yay EL-skahr day]
> Tagalog: *mahal kita* [mah-HAHL kee-TAH]
> Turkish: *seni seviyorum* [seh-nee seh-vee-YOR-oom]

Terms of Endearment

I f one were to draw up a taxonomy of pet names or terms of endearment from around the world, there would be several large categories. Chief among them would be these groups: delicious things to eat (especially sweet ones, although *ham bone* can be used as a term of endearment in Southern American English, and *mon petit chou*, or 'my little cabbage,' is a common and affectionate French pet name); animals, especially cute or cuddly ones (*my little bird, my honey bunny*); parts of the body (*my heart*), flowers (*my rose, sweet pea*), and astronomical objects (*you are the sun, the moon, and the stars*).

The idea of smallness is also important in pet names, and in English it seems that almost anything with a diminutive suffix can be used as an endearment: lamb*kin*, duck*ling*, dear*ie* (or ladd*ie*), ny*let* (an obsolete word meaning 'little eye'). And if *nylet* doesn't serve, there are plenty of other obsolete endearments waiting for another turn: *bulchin* or *bulkin* (bull-calf), *chuckaby* (perhaps from *chickie*), *cow-huby* (calf, again), *flitter-mouse* (bat), *frisko* (maybe from "frisky person"), *fubs* (small chubby person), *golpol* (perhaps meaning "golden-haired"), *miting* (little mite), *muskin* (pretty face), *picaroon* (thief), *pinkany* (little pink eye— "pink eye" here meaning 'small' or 'winking,' not conjunctivitis), *powsoddy* (possibly from a kind of pudding), *slawsy-gawsy* (from where, nobody knows).

Of course, anything can serve as a pet name if it's said with the right emphasis: how about *cupcake pants* and *cheese teeth*, both actual examples taken from people not only foolhardy enough to use those particular endearments, but also brave enough to post them on the Internet. Which brings to mind another important aspect of pet names: between two people, they're a sign of love; in front of a third, they're an occasion for embarrassment. Many a person enchanted at being called *snookums* at home is tormented by it in public.

A more cryptic way to express endearments is through the use of acronyms (which long predated text-messaging, being used in servicemen's letters). Some are obviously acronyms, including *shmily*, 'see how much I love you,' *flak*, 'fond love and kisses,' the more familiar *swak*, 'sealed with a kiss,' and the much longer (and probably only used by schoolgirls) *swalcakws*, 'sealed with a lick, 'cause a kiss wouldn't stick.' There's also the half-acronym, half-symbolic *lxxx*, 'love and kisses.' Other acronyms masqueraded as other words: *Holland*, for instance, was 'hope our love lasts and never dies,' *Italy*, 'I trust and love you,' or, more awkwardly, 'I truly always love you,' and *Burma*, 'be undressed ready, my angel.' (That last reminiscent of Napoleon's famous and apocryphal-sounding direction to Josephine: "Arriving in three days. Don't wash.") More cryptic still is the ham-radio *88*, which stands for 'love and kisses' (the tamer *73* is just 'best regards').

un tremendo bizcocho (Spanish)
[oon treh-MEN-doh bees-KOH-tchoh]

If a man is described as a 'tremendous cupcake' in Spanish, it doesn't imply anything about his masculinity—quite the opposite. It means he's really, really cute. A great big sweet thing, in fact!

khordani (Persian)
[khor-dan-EE]

This word translates as 'eatable'—calling someone *khordani* is like calling someone *delicious* in English, only stronger. The affectionate pet name *hooloo*, 'peach,' is another pet name that compares a loved one with something beautiful and good to eat.

min lilla sockertopp (Swedish)
[meen LEEL-lah SOK-er-top]

Literally 'my little sugar top,' this old-fashioned Swedish phrase goes back to the days when sugar came in cones. You would then use tongs to break off a bit of sugar to sweeten your food or drink, in the same way that your lover, or *sockertopp*, would make your life a bit sweeter.

muru (Finnish)
[MOO-roo]

Muru literally translates as 'crumb.' This metaphor is also used in Swedish, where those sweet nothings that you whisper in your lover's ear include *tårtsmula* ('cake crumb') and *sockerpulla* ('sugar crumb').

mon petit chou (French)
[monh p'tee SHOO]
Some terms of affection are quite straightforward: *mon chou à la crème*, 'my cream puff' and *mon sucre d'orge*, 'my barley sugar' both make sense; they're quite like the English *honey*, *babycakes*, or *sweetie pie*. But why *mon petit chou*, literally 'my little cabbage,' should be a fond name for one's beloved, only the French know.

Zuckerschnecke (German)
[TSOOK-er-shnek-uh]
In English, calling your girlfriend a snail might not get you a warm reception, but in German 'snail' is regularly used to refer to a lovely girl. Adding *Zucker*, 'sugar,' just makes it sweeter.

amar shona (Bengali)
[ah-mahr SHOH-nah]
Shona in Bengali literally means 'gold,' but in the expression *amar shona* it means "darling." Other Bengali terms of endearment also follow this theme: *amar pran* means 'my life' or 'my soul'; *amar mon* translates as 'my mind'; and *amar dhon* means 'my wealth.'

skat (Danish)
[skaht]
Skat, the most common endearment in Danish, means 'treasure.' However, *skat* also can also mean "tax," so make sure you keep your contexts straight!

mahal (Indonesian/Tagalog)
[MAH-hahl/mah-HAHL]
In both Indonesian and Tagalog, *mahal* means 'dear,' both as a term of endearment and to mean "expensive." It is derived from

Sanskrit, where the word is also used to mean "great"
or "important."

zlato (Czech)
[ZLAH-toh]
Zlato, 'gold,' is used to express how special someone is to you.
The diminutive *zlatičko* is even more affectionate. Meaning 'little
gold,' it combines the idea of something precious with the idea of
something small—two traditional ways of expressing affection.

cariad bach (Welsh)
[KAHR-yahd BAKH]
Cariad translates as 'my heart,' while *bach* means 'dear,' 'beloved,'
or 'little one.' Together, the phrase means "my little love."

carissimo/carissima (Italian)
[kah-REES-see-moh/kah-REES-see-mah]
Carissimo/a means 'dearest' or 'most dear,' and can also be
translated as "darling."

thîi rák (Thai)
[tee RAHK]
Thîi rak is 'dear' or 'darling'; 'lover' is *khon rák*; 'sweetheart' is *khûu
rák*. *Rák*, unsurprisingly, is 'love.'

Schatzi (German)
[SHAHT-see]
One German magazine estimated that about seventy percent of
all German couples use a *Kosename*, or pet name, with each
other. One of the most popular is *Schatz* (or one of its many
variations: *Schatzi, Schätzchen, Schätzelchen, Schätzlein*), which
translates literally as 'treasure.'

je bent om op te vreten (Dutch)
[yay bent om op tuh VRAY-tuh]
The Dutch phrase means "you are adorable" and is used mainly to describe women, babies, and small animals.

mi perla (Spanish)
[mee PAIR-lah]
Literally, 'my pearl.' Other Spanish endearments include *mis ojos,* 'my eyes,' and *mi reina,* 'my queen.' Argentines call their boyfriends and girlfriends *el/la filito/a,* 'little knife,' and Chileans use *el/la pololo/a,* 'bumblebee,' but possibly the most common is plain *querido/a,* 'dear.'

schnickelfritz (American English)
This word means "a naughty (but cute) little boy," but is also used to mean "sweetheart." It might come from a German dialect word *Schnickel,* meaning 'little boy's penis,' added to the name *Fritz.*

sayang (Tagalog)
[SAH-yang]
Although usually *sayang* is translated into English as "what a waste!" the word connotes a deep sadness or longing for something lost, and, when used as an endearment, means something like "love," "sweetheart," or "dear." The Korean word *han* has a similar feeling.

-chan (Japanese)
[tchahn]
Pet names are used less in Japan than elsewhere. However, some couples use nicknames derived by abbreviating their first name and adding the suffix *-chan,* which signifies endearment. So, for

Till Death Do You Part

It's funny that marriage, a state that can be entered into just by the saying of two little words, has so many phrases to discuss it—most of them uncomplimentary, or at the very least, cynical. In Yorkshire, those that marry are said to have *tied a knot with their tongue that they cannot untie with their teeth*. The Scots say that married people are like rats in a trap, *fain to get ithers in, but fain to be out themselves*. The French have *le mariage est comme une forteresse assiégée; ceux qui sont dehors veulent y entrer et ceux qui sont dedans en sortir*: 'Marriage is like a besieged fortress: those who are in want to get out, and those who out want to get in.' Socrates himself, when asked if a man should marry, said "Whichever you do, you will repent it."

Although, if you do marry, the ideal is to marry for love, it's *long ere four bare legs heat in a bed*, say the Scots—it's better to have money too. Not necessarily *cupboard love* (out-and-out gold digging), but it's said that a *kiss and a drink of water is a tasteless breakfast*. (When a younger woman marries a rich older man, his *auld brass will buy her a new pan*.) The French have *Amour fait rage, mais argent fait mariage*: 'love makes rage, but money makes marriage.' For richer or poorer, marriage is often seen as fated: *marriage and hanging go by destiny*. The Scots have *a man may woo where he will, but must wed where he's weird* (fated) and the Irish have *marriage comes unawares, like a soot-drop* (drop of rain).

When you marry, you should do it right away: *Opleygn iz nor gut for kez, ober nit far a khasene* is a Yiddish proverb meaning "delay is good for cheese, but not for a wedding." Especially if

the bride *took a stone up her ear* or *cracked her pitcher* before marriage, meaning there's a risk of her *spraining her ankle* (becoming an unmarried mother).

Of course, once you're a wife, you're fodder for jokes: the domineering wife *has a man's head under her girdle* or has *got round a man's neck-hole*; either way, she has an undue influence over her husband. A man coming home to an angry wife was told to *throw your cap in first*; the Scots say that a man who is yelled at by his wife *gets his meat in a riven cog*. (A *riven cog* is a broken bucket.) If the yelling gets too burdensome, though, the man might *go visit his uncle*—leave soon after marrying. Conversely, there's a Chinese proverb *da shi teng, ma shi ai*, 'smacking is fondness and scolding is love,' and a Yiddish one *der ershter broygez iz der bester broygez*, 'the first fight is the best fight.'

Despite everything, the Chinese proverb *haoshi duo mo* probably has it best: "it takes many twists and turns to make a good marriage."

example, *Takeshi* becomes *Take-chan*, while *Hanako* would be *Hana-chan*.

cucciola mia (Italian)
[KOOTCH-oh-lah MEE-ah]
This Italian phrase is literally 'my little animal,' a pet name that implies someone is your pet!

golubka (Russian)
[gah-LOOP-kuh]
Russian is awash with phrases that liken one's loved one with baby animals—cute, cuddly things that need one's protection. *Golubka* is 'little dove' (*golub' moi sizokrylyi* is 'my blue-winged dove,' for extra emphasis). Other common pet names include *moi kotik*, 'my kitten,' *zaika moja*, 'my little wild hare,' and *ptichka moya*, 'my little bird.'

Knuddelbär (German)
[K'NUD-uhl-bair]
Literally 'cuddle bear,' this is not quite like the English *teddy bear*; it connotes not just softness and sweetness, but protective strength, as well.

tausi wangu (Swahili)
[tah-OO-see WAHNG-goo]
A Swahili-speaking woman might call the man in her life *tausi wangu*, 'my peacock,' implying that he is handsome; a Swahili-speaking man would call his sweetheart *waridi wangu*, or 'my rose,' referring to her beauty.

ma biche (French)
[mah BEESH]

Ma biche means 'my doe,' an image that recalls the *Song of Solomon*: "my beloved is a like a roe (deer) or a young hart." *Mon canard* means 'my duck,' which, in the form *ducks*, should be familiar to English speakers. *Ma puce*, literally 'my flea,' is not so familiar, but comes from the idea of fond attachment to someone rather small.

topolina (Italian)
[toh-poh-LEE-nah]

Topolina is another small, cute animal word; this one is 'little mouse.' Italian endearments also include *passerotto*, 'little sparrow' and *patatino*, 'little potato.'

churri (Spanish)
[TCHOO-ree]

Churri literally translates as 'my squeezy.' Perhaps it is used when someone is nice to hold?

fofinho/fofinha (Portuguese)
[foh-FEE-nyoh / foh-FEE-nyah]

A warm and enveloping term of affection, *fofo* means 'soft and light' or 'fluffy.' It can be used to describe an extremely comfortable bed or a light and airy cake. It connotes that being with your *fofinho* makes you feel comfortable and at ease.

dob o' goody (American English)

A dialect word for a sweetheart; perhaps from *dob*, 'lump' and *goody*, 'anything good.'

gordito (Spanish)
[gor-DEE-toh]
In El Salvador, lovers call each other *gordito* or *gordita*, which literally translates as 'little fat one.' It comes from the name of a Mexican dish made of dough stuffed with cheese, pork, chicken, or beans. Italian has a similar term *ciccio* or *ciccia*, meaning 'flesh' or 'fat.' Perhaps the connotation is not so much one of size as of savor.

Pummel (German)
[PUM-uhl]
Pummel literally translates as 'chubby one,' and conveys the German belief that chubby people are more *gemütlich*. *Gemütlich* is often translated as 'cosy,' 'snug,' or 'comfortable.' If someone calls you *Pummel*, they feel comfortable, relaxed, easy, and at home with you.

coccolissima/coccolone (Italian)
[kok-ko-LEESS-see-mah/kok-ko-LOH-nay]
These are sweet Italian terms for a person whom you'd like to snuggle with in bed. It comes from *coccolare*, a word used to describe a mother cuddling a baby. *Coccolo* means 'cuddly.' It is often coupled with *dormigliona/dormiglione*, meaning 'she/he who is always sleeping.' *Coccolissima* plus *dormigliona* equals long Sunday mornings among the pillows and under the covers.

luce dei miei occhi (Italian)
[LOO-tchay day mee-ay OK-kee]
This phrase is literally translated as 'light of my eyes,' but is probably more like the English "you are my sunshine." In the English phrase *apple of my eye*, the *apple* is the pupil; the pupil was thought of as a hard, round object, like an apple.

solntse moe nenaglyadnoe (Russian)
[SAWN-tsuh mah-YAW ni-nah-GLYAHD-nuh-yuh]
Literally meaning 'my sun that I can't stop looking at,' this seems overly extravagant to English speakers. The affectionate *myj nezhnii luchik sveta*, or 'my tender little ray of light,' is more like our "you are my sunshine." Romanian has a similar endearment, *soarele meu*, meaning 'my sun.' In English, someone "lights up your life"; in Russian and Romanian, they light the whole world.

zarya moya yasnaya (Russian)
[zah-RYAH mah-YAH YAHS-nuh-yuh]
Literally 'my bright dawn,' this is a very intimate Russian endearment, perhaps best spoken in bed, first thing in the morning?

chaudvin ka chand (Urdu)
[TCHOW-dvin kah TCHUHND]
This endearment has been used both as the title of a Bollywood feature and a hit song; it's literally '14th day of the month' and means "you are my full moon."

meng.gàn (Cantonese)
[meng-gahn]
Meng.gàn is translated as "root of my life," or something on which everything depends. A similar sentiment can be found

Rings, stones, and symbols

For a token of love to be truly effective, it must pass several tests. It must be deeply symbolic, preferably in an allusive, rather than a direct way; it must be able to be hidden; and it must be easy to send. There is a reason that lovers do not, in the main, send each other large marble elephants.

The ring has always been a favorite love token, passing as it does all the tests above. In the late Middle Ages, a particular kind of love-ring, the *gimmel* (used by the Greeks and Romans as well) had a resurgence in popularity. *Gimmel* comes from *gemelli*, meaning twins, and the rings were made of two, three, or even four bands, which fit together on the finger as one ring. Sometimes a gimmel ring was also a *fede* ring, which had a clasp shaped like miniature hands, which interwined when the ring was worn, and symbolized fidelity and "plighted troth." Gimmel rings could also be worn separately, each person taking one, and, while wearing them, think of the time when both the rings and the wearers would be reunited.

Robert Herrick wrote of a gimmel ring:

Thous sent'st to me a true love knot; but I
return a ring of jimmals, to imply
Thy love had one knot, mine a triple tye.

(The love knot was a double-looped bow, or a knot of two loops intertwined, and symbolized true love.)

The amethyst
was once considered
to be the precious
stone that symbolized
true love. The legend
went that a beautiful
nymph (as if there were
any other kind) was being
pursued by Bacchus, and to protect
the nymph a goddess turned her into an amethyst. Bacchus,
despite his disappointment, gave the amethyst its deep purple
color, after his other love, wine. Opals have often been
considered highly unlucky, and thus unsuitable for engagement
or marriage rings. In spite of this, Queen Victoria gave all her
daughters opals at their marriages (much to the delight of her
opal-mining Australian subjects).

The giving of a ring made of rushes was once considered to
be enough to make a legal marriage, without any need for
priests or witnesses. (This custom is referred to in *All's Well That
Ends Well*.) Unfortunately, not everyone shared this belief, and
many women were left with a rush ring and no husband.

Perhaps the most unusual wedding ring custom is that of the
Basotho, where, at the wedding, the father of the bride butchers
an ox. He cuts off the dewlap and divides it into two strips: one
for the bride's wrist and one for the groom's, which they then
wear to show that they are bound to one another.

in the phrase *sàm.gàwn*, which means 'heart and liver'—used when your loved one is so important that you cannot live without them.

jegar (Persian)
[djeh-GAR]
Jegar, literally 'liver,' is a common term of endearment in Persian—and implies that your sweetheart is something you can't live without.

tzieri mou (Greek)
[dzee-AIR-ee-moo]
Literally 'my liver,' this is used with the same affection as "my love" would be in English. In many cultures, the liver is considered the seat of the affections, in the way that the heart is considered to be the organ responsible for love in English. The word *tzieri* comes from the Turkish *ciger*, which in turn comes from the Persian *jegar*; they all mean 'liver.'

wo de xingan baobei (Chinese)
[woh-duh sheen-gahn bow-bay]
While this phrase translates as "my precious darling/treasure," if you look at each character individually it becomes 'my heart–liver precious cowrie shell.' *Xingan*, or 'heart-liver,' is a traditional expression of deep affection for one's partner or child, presumably because these two organs are vital for life. *Baobei*, or 'cowrie shells,' make the phrase even more expressive: Cowrie shells were once used as currency in China, so using this word to refer to your partner shows just how dear they are to you.

poepie (Dutch)
[POO-pee]

Poepie is literally 'small shit.' Another Dutch pet name, *scheetje*, is literally 'small fart.' Both are used mean "love" or "darling" and are terms that you would happily address to your lover (should you both speak Dutch). One language's endearment can be another's insult!

bookie-sug (American English)

A dialect word for "sweetheart." *The Dictionary of American Regional English* shows it was given to them by a 68-year-old informant from South Carolina, who laughed after saying it.

moosh bekhoradet (Persian)
[MOOSH BAY-kho-rad-et]

When you have run out of traditional endearments, you may want to borrow an odd turn of phrase from Persian, *moosh bekhoradet*, or 'May a mouse eat you.'

sonqochallay, urpichallay, sonqo suwa, ch'aska ñawi (Quechua)
[son-kho-TCHAHL-yah-ee, ur-pee-TCHAHL-yah-ee, SON-kho SOO-wah, TCHAHSS-kah NYAH-wee]

This long, romantic phrase means 'dear heart, my little dove, thief of hearts, eyes like the stars.' One gets the idea.

hartendief (Dutch)
[HAHR-tuhn-deef]

This adjective literally means 'thief of my heart.' English only has heartbreakers, not heart-thieves (although we can say someone "stole my heart.")

Word Finder

A

a minha cara metade, *Portuguese* **74**
a outra metade da laranja,
      Portuguese **74**
abrasarse vivo, *Spanish* **45**
ag briseadh na gcos i ndiaidh duine,
      Irish **64**
alamnaka, *Ulwa* **80**
als een blok voor iemand vallen,
      Dutch **15**
amar shona, *Bengali* **93**
amoroso, *Italian* **32**
ana l-`alīl w–inta d–dawā, *Arabic* **69**
`ashiqa, *Arabic* **53**
aufreißen, *German* **34**
avoir le béguin pour quelqu'un,
      French **26**
avoir un coeur d'artichaut, *French* **38**
avskjed på grått papir, *Norwegian* **64**

B

basbasa, *Arabic* **20**
bashert, *Yiddish* **22**
beber los vientos por alguien,
      Spanish **64**
bercumbu-cumbuan, *Indonesian* **39**
beth amdanon ni'n mynd lan llofft?,
      Welsh **48**
bi yue xiu hua, *Chinese* **33**
billet-doux, *French/English* **32**
blixtförälskelse, *Swedish* **14**
bookie-sug, *American English* **105**

C

când dragoste nu e (este), nimic nu e
      (este), *Romanian* **71**
cargar el arpa, *Latin American
      Spanish* **71**

cariad bach, *Welsh* **94**
carissimo/carissima, *Italian* **94**
cavoli riscaldati, *Italian* **68**
-chan, *Japanese* **95**
chaudvin ka chand, *Urdu* **101**
chen pian chih yan mo t'ing,
      Chinese **86**
churri, *Spanish* **99**
ci facciamo della storie, *Italian* **53**
cinta monyet, *Indonesian* **27**
coccolissima/coccolone, *Italian* **100**
colpo di fulmine, *Italian* **14**
comerle la oreja, *Spanish* **34**
cucciola mia, *Italian* **98**

D

dar calabazas a alguien, *Spanish* **62**
dare il pacco a qualcuno, *Italian* **56**
di libe kumt noch der khasene,
      Yiddish **85**
die Bettgeschichte, *German* **52**
dob o'goody, *American English* **99**
dor, *Romanian* **70**
dostac czarną polewkę, *Polish* **57**
dowret begardam, *Persian* **84**
du hast mir den Kopf verdreht,
      German **44**
duo ru qing wang, *Chinese* **46**

E

é boa/bom como o milho,
      Portuguese **35**
een beschuitje met hem willen eten,
      Dutch **39**
een blauwtje lopen, *Dutch* **60**
el ha dado el flechazo, *Spanish* **14**
empiernado/a, *Venezuelan Spanish* **86**
entyi-pentyi, *Hungarian* **49**

es funkt/knistert zwischen zwei
  Menschen, *German* **23**
es vercht mir finster in die egen,
  Yiddish **65**
essere sotto un treno, *Italian* **64**
estar tísico/consumido de amor,
  Spanish **45**
estoy hecho/hecha polvo, *Spanish* **61**

F

faire la bouche en coeur, *French* **35**
faire la coquette, *French* **40**
fare il filo a qualcuno, *Italian* **21**
fartshadet, *Yiddish* **28**
fofinho/fofinha, *Portuguese* **99**
fordolked of luf-daungere, *Middle
  English* **61**
Frauendienst, *German* **32**
fusto, *Italian* **40**

G

get one's nose open, *English* **27**
golubka, *Russian* **98**
gordito, *Spanish* **100**
grá mo chroí thú, *Irish* **81**
gua sayang lu, *Indonesian* **80**

H

há mouro na costa, *Portuguese* **44**
hacer manitas, *Spanish* **48**
hacer un gancho, *Spanish* **33**
hamnafasam baash, *Persian* **84**
hana kalakalai, *Hawaiian* **53**
hartendief, *Dutch* **105**
hiza o majieru, *Japanese* **34**
ho preso una cotta, *Italian* **26**
hodestups forelsket, *Norwegian* **16**
honeyfuggler, *American English* **40**
hubbak yidhawwibni, *Arabic* **84**

I

i kardia mou ekhi gini thripsala,
  Greek **60**
I love you, *English* **89**
ich hab mich in dich vernarrt,
  German **28**

ich liebe dich, *German* **85**
igg, *AAVE* **63**
ik zou je op kunnen vreten/je bent
  om op te vreten, *Dutch* **44**
ir embalado hacia alguien, *Spanish* **40**

J

j'ai besoin de tes baisers, *French* **75**
je bent om op te vreten, *Dutch* **95**
je t'ai dans la peau/tu me colles à la
  peau, *French* **47**
jegar, *Persian* **104**
jemandem einen Korb geben,
  German **63**
jemandem schlägt das Herz bis zum
  Hals, *German* **23**
jemanden mit Haut und Haar
  aufessen wollen, *German* **45**
jeong, *Korean* **80**
jō ga fukai, *Japanese* **65**
jō ga utsuru, *Japanese* **29**

K

kalverliefde, *Dutch* **27**
kamaki, *Greek* **39**
khatereto mikham, *Persian* **84**
khordani, *Persian* **92**
Knuddelbär, *German* **98**
kutimunaykin, llakiymanta mana
  wañunaypaq, *Quechua* **68**

L

la drague, *French* **38**
la petite mort, *French* **52**
llevar a alguien al huerto, *Spanish* **57**
ligar, *Spanish* **38**
luce dei miei occhi, *Italian* **100**
luddevedu, *Dutch* **60**
luí le chéile, *Irish* **52**
lyubit' tebya slozhno, ne lyubit'—
  nevozmozhno, *Russian* **65**

M

mă sting fără iubirea ei/lui,
  Romanian **61**
ma biche, *French* **99**

mabuk cinta, *Indonesian* **17**
mahal, *Indonesian / Tagalog* **93**
mamihlapinatapai, *Yaghan* **27**
mapenzi ni maua huchanua na
    kunyauka, *Swahili* **70**
masihlalisane, *Zulu* **87**
me traes de nalgas, *Mexican*
    Spanish **16**
mei mu chuan qing, *Chinese* **38**
melaut, *Indonesian* **48**
meng.gàn, *Cantonese* **101**
mero-mero, *Japanese* **17**
mi perla, *Spanish* **95**
mi-a rămas sufletul la tine,
    Romanian **22**
mi-ai frânt inima, *Romanian* **60**
min lilla sockertopp, *Swedish* **92**
misschien moeten we dan toch
    maar trouwen, *Dutch* **87**
mitn gantsn hartsn, *Yiddish* **79**
mizgatisya, *Ukrainian* **86**
mne tak sladok tvoy plen, *Russian* **69**
mon petit chou, *French* **93**
moosh bekhoradet, *Persian* **105**
mune kyun, *Japanese* **22**
mune o kogasu, *Japanese* **22**
muru, *Finnish* **92**
myliu, *Lithuanian* **88**

N

na tebe soshelsa klinom belyi svet,
    Russian **81**
naazet-ra beram / naazat-ra beravam,
    Persian **46**
nagligi-, *Eastern Canadian Inuktitut* **60**
ndege wangu karuka mtini,
    Swahili **69**
netsu wo ageru, *Japanese* **26**
níl aon leigheas ar an ngrá ach pósadh,
    Irish **87**
no comerse una rosca, *Spanish* **57**

O

obicham te do bolka, *Bulgarian* **79**
òk hàk, *Thai* **62**
omae hyaku made washa kujuku

made, tomo ni shiraga no haeru
    made, *Japanese* **86**
on s'est mis à poil, *French* **48**
onguboy, *Boro* **78**

P

patah cinta, *Indonesian* **61**
patimă, *Romanian* **46**
pehli nazar mein pyaar ho gaya,
    Hindi **15**
pelar la pava, *Spanish* **33**
pitsounakia, *Greek* **48**
plámásach, *Irish* **45**
poepie, *Dutch* **105**
poisoned on, *American English* **23**
pokata, *Finnish* **39**
poser un lapin à quelqu'un, *French* **56**
prendere una sbandata per qualcuno,
    Italian **26**
Pummel, *German* **100**

Q

qing ren yan li chu xishi, *Chinese* **88**
qiubo, *Chinese* **21**
qorbaanat beravam, fedaayat
    beshavam, *Persian* **75**

R

razliubit, *Russian* **65**
red in the comb, *American English* **53**
retkahtaa, *Finnish* **17**
rimorchiare, *Italian* **33**
rouler un patin, *French* **47**
rwy'n dwli arnat ti, *Welsh* **29**
rwy'n dy garu di, *Welsh* **78**

S

s'envoyer en l'air, *French* **49**
saudade, *Portuguese* **70**
sayang, *Tagalog* **95**
Schatzi, *German* **94**
schnickelfritz, *American English* **95**
Schnitte, *German* **35**
Schwarm, *German* **41**
scopare, *Italian* **49**
se prendre une veste, *French* **63**

sein Blick ging mir durch Mark und
    Bein, *German* **20**
seykhl, *Yiddish* **46**
shindemo ii wa, *Japanese* **79**
sich Hals über Kopf verlieben,
    German **17**
sine ce elong, *Drehu* **88**
siúl amach le duine, *Irish* **41**
skat, *Danish* **93**
šmrkati se, *Serbo-Croat* **15**
solntse moe nenaglyadnoe,
    Russian **101**
sonqochallay, urpichallay, sonqo suwa,
    ch'aska ñawi, *Quechua* **105**
spasibo chto ty est' na svete!,
    Russian **74**
stati na ludi kamen, *Serbo-Croat* **16**
sufrir un ataque de cuernos,
    Latin American Spanish **65**
suki de tamaranai, *Japanese* **28**

T
ta de zi hen piao liang, *Chinese* **63**
tá mo chroí istigh inti, *Irish* **78**
tausi wangu, *Swahili* **98**
te adoro, *Spanish* **75**
tener el corazón en la mano,
    Spanish **62**
tha gràdh agam ort, *Scots Gaelic* **78**
tha se fao, *Greek* **45**
thîi rák, *Thai* **94**
ti voglio bene, *Italian* **85**
tipyn o foi/tipyn o ferch, *Welsh* **41**
tirare il bidone a qualcuno, *Italian* **56**
tirarsela, *Italian* **57**
topolina, *Italian* **99**
traer azorrillado/a,
    Mexican Spanish **86**
tragado como media de cartero,
    Spanish **20**
tsebrochen, *Yiddish* **62**
ty menya prigubil, *Russian* **49**
tzieri mou, *Greek* **104**

U
udari me sliapata nedelia, *Bulgarian* **21**
un beso del, *Spanish* **47**
un coup de foudre, *French* **14**
un tremendo bizcocho, *Spanish* **92**

V
va voir ailleurs si j'y suis, *French* **56**
vanha suola janottaa, *Finnish* **68**
vliuben do ushi, *Bulgarian* **20**
voetje vrijen, *Dutch* **52**
vzema mi uma, *Bulgarian* **26**

W
wewe ndiyo barafu wa moyo wangu,
    Swahili **81**
wewe ni wangu tu, *Swahili* **84**
wo de xingan baobei, *Chinese* **104**

X
xiang si, *Chinese* **69**
xiyyet, *Dardja* **35**

Y
ya poteryal pokoy i rassudok,
    Russian **29**
ya soshel s uma ot lyubvi, *Russian* **29**
ya toboy bolna/bolen, *Russian* **68**
ya vlubilsya bez oglyadki, *Russian* **15**
yasashii, *Japanese* **47**
yi jian zhong qing, *Chinese* **15**
yi wang qing shen, *Chinese* **79**

Z
zarya moya yasnaya, *Russian* **101**
zlato, *Czech* **94**
Zuckerschnecke, *German* **93**

Acknowledgments

Mark Abley, *Spoken Here*, William Heinemann, London, 2003.

Petra Baeumer, Miriam Gertzen, and **Christina Riesenweber** and for contributions to German words.

Zhaleh Beheshti, Somayyeh Jaferi, Azadeh Karimian, and **Marzia Nazari** for contributions and review to Persian words.

Berlitz, *Hide This Spanish Book*, Berlitz, 2004.

Emma Britton and **Benjamin Zimmer** for contributions to Indonesian words.

Miguel Calderon Aviles, Chelo Herrerias Rodriguez, Abel Jimenez Ramon, Lameen Souag and **Olga Muñoz** for contributions to words in Spanish and Spanish dialects.

Slavomir Ceplo for contributions to Arabic words.

Ekaterina Chekulaeva and **Slav Vasilevski** for contributions to Russian words.

Dr. Qing Cao, Senior Lecturer and Programme Leader in Chinese at Liverpool John Moores University, United Kingdom, for his contributions to and clarification of Chinese words.

Maggie Chijenga for contributions to Swahili words.

Fred Ciporen for review and contributions to Yiddish words.

Julie Coleman, *Love, Sex, and Marriage: A Historical Thesaurus,* Rodopi, 1999.

Donna Condon for contributions to Irish words.

Peter Constantine and **Soe Tjen Marching**, *Making Out in Indonesian,* Tuttle, 2004.

Nan Craig for contributions to Welsh words.

Ray Daniels, *Making Out in Chinese,* Tuttle, 2003.

Karoliina Elder and **Tuomas Sorjamaa** for review contributions to Finnish words.

Francesca Ficai, Fabienne Gasparini, and **Valérie Le Plouhinec** for review and contributions to French words.

Francesca Ficai for contributions to Italian words.

Takuka Fujiyoshi and **Wakako Hirose** for review and contributions to Japanese words.

Sylvia Gaitas and **Ana Paula Romão** for review and contributions to Portuguese words.

Todd Geers, Erika Geers, and **Glen McCabe**, *Making Out in Japanese,* Tuttle, 2004.

Daniella Gobetti, *Dictionary of Italian Slang and Expressions,* Barrons, 1999.

Andrew Horvat, *Japanese Beyond Words: How to Walk and Talk like a Native Speaker,* Stone Bridge Press, California, 2000.

Gunnel Klingener and **Robert Sarvik** for review and contributions to Swedish words.

Martine Koelemeijer for contributions to Dutch words.

Boyé Lafayette De Mente, *The Japanese Have a Word for It*, Passport Books, Illinois, 1994.

Anna Malaos for contributions to Greek words.

Mamiko Murakami, *Love, Hate, and Everything in Between: Expressing Emotions in Japanese*, Kodansha, 2002.

Ian Pickup and **Rod Hares**, *Streetwise French Dictionary/Thesaurus: The User-Friendly Guide to French Slang and Idioms*, McGraw-Hill, 2002.

Nadja Race and **Neda Stefanovic** for contributions to Serbo-Croatian words.

Branimira Radoslavova for contributions to Bulgarian words.

Nadja Rizzuti, *Hide This Italian Book*, Berlitz, 2005.

Howard Rheingold, *They Have a Word for It*, Sarabande Books, Louisville, Kentucky, 2000.

Leo Rosten, *The New Joys of Yiddish*, Arrow Books, Random House Group Limited, 2003.

Eve-Alice Roustang-Stoller, *Hide This French Book,* Berlitz, 2004.

Robert Sarvik for contributions to Romanian words.

Stina Smemo for contributions to Norwegian words.

Jennifer Speake (ed.), *The Oxford Dictionary of Foreign Words and Phrases*, Oxford University Press, New York, 2005.

Henry Strutz, *Dictionary of German Slang,* Barrons, 2000.

Jess Tauber for contributions to the Yahgan words.

William Tegg, *The Knot Tied: Marriage Ceremonies of All Nations*, Singing Tree Press (facsimile), 1970.

Edward Topol, *Dermo! The Real Russian Tolstoy Never Used*, Plume, 1997.

Brenda Wegmann and **Mary McVey Gill**, *Streetwise Spanish*, McGraw-Hill 1998.

Jolita Vadopalaite for contributions to Lithuanian words.

The publisher would also like to thank the following people for their contributions to this book: Philippa Crane, Claire Dunn, Jane Eastwood, Christopher Heaton, Erin King, Silvia Langford, and Toria Leitch. Your input into the research and production of this book was highly appreciated.

The author would like to thank Christopher J. Moore, Ben Zimmer, Orion Montoya, Katie Haegele, Luanne von Schneidemesser, and *DARE,* Laura Dickey, Grant Barrett, Joseph Gerharz, Google Book Search and Google Scholar, Valerie Sultan, Victor Golla, Michael Fortescue, and John Myhill for their help, support, or (in some cases) forbearance. Also, many thanks to Stephen Dodson, our heroic copyeditor, without whom this book could not have been completed, and without whom I would not have even considered beginning.

Every effort has been made to obtain permissions for material used in this book and to contact the copyright holders. The publisher apologizes for any omissions and would welcome contact from copyright holders for correction in subsequent editions.

ek het jou life

maite zaitut

inhobbok

i love you

es tevi milu!

minä rakastan sinua

mahal kita

kocham cie

HICKMANS